Transatlantic Relations

CHATHAM HOUSE PAPERS

An International Security Programme Publication
Programme Director: Professor Sir Laurence Martin

The Royal Institute of International Affairs, at Chatham House in London, has provided an impartial forum for discussion and debate on current international issues for 75 years. Its resident research fellows, specialized information resources, and range of publications, conferences, and meetings span the fields of international politics, economics, and security. The Institute is independent of government.

Chatham House Papers are short monographs on current policy problems which have been commissioned by the RIIA. In preparing the papers, authors are advised by a study group of experts convened by the RIIA, and publication of a paper indicates that the Institute regards it as an authoritative contribution to the public debate. The Institute does not, however, hold opinions of its own; the views expressed in this publication are the responsibility of the author.

CHATHAM HOUSE PAPERS

Transatlantic Relations

Sharing ideals and costs

Beatrice Heuser

THE ROYAL INSTITUTE
OF INTERNATIONAL
AFFAIRS

Pinter
A Cassell Imprint
Wellington House, 125 Strand, London WC2R 0BB, United Kingdom

First published in 1996

British Library Cataloguing in Publication Data
A CIP catalogue record for this book is available from the British Library

Library of Congress Cataloging in Publication Data
A CIP catalogue record for this book is available from the Library of Congress

ISBN 1-85567-355-X (Paperback)
     1-85567-354-1 (Hardback)

Typeset by Koinonia Limited
Printed and bound in Great Britain by
Biddles Limited, Guildford and King's Lynn

Contents

Contents

Tables

Acknowledgments

In the preparation of this study, I have greatly benefited from generous help from many quarters. Above all, I must thank Professors Jack Spence and Trevor Taylor, and of course Sir Laurence Martin, for their advice. The Chatham House study group which was convened was most helpful, and there are a number of individuals to whom I owe many thanks for their patient comments on my draft paper, and the time they must have taken over it. I learnt a great deal from the discussion process which was conducted in this way, and am very honoured by the attention this paper was given. Needless to say, none of those referred to bear any responsibility for the remaining defects of this book or for its argument, and the views expressed here are the author's own, and should not be taken to reflect the opinion of any government or institution.

I very gratefully acknowledge the financial and also the brilliant organizational help I received from the Canadian government, including a fact-finding mission to Canada, without which this paper would be much poorer. In particular James R. Wright, Dr Rob McRae and Christine O'Neill deserve my warmest thanks for their help. It gave me great pleasure and intellectual stimulation to learn a little (and read a great deal) about this fascinating country of which I had known very little before.

I also want to thank Charles Peacock from the US Embassy in London, who now as on previous occasions has furnished me with large amounts of documentation and much general advice as well as detailed reflections on individual issues. My warm thanks are due also Margaret May and the Chatham House publications department, and to Emma Matanle, one of my star pupils, to whom I am greatly indebted for her help with this paper.

Acknowledgments

I would like to dedicate this paper to my North American friends: Carol, Robin and Gail, my first childhood playmates, to whom I owed my American accent; Susan Dolman Webb, Dr Alice Hill, Dr Michele Margetts, my fellow-students in London; David Angell, Christopher Cook, William George, who introduced me to the American Far North; and my academic colleagues Dr Catherine Kelleher, Dr Edwina Campbell, Professor David Yost and many others, whose wonderful sense of fun and sharing has made working with them so refreshing.

August 1996   Beatrice Heuser

Chapter 1

Introduction

This Chatham House Paper is intended to examine the role, the importance, the limitations and the possibilities of transatlantic relations in the narrow sense of the term: that is, relations between the United States and Canada on one side of the Atlantic, and their NATO allies on the other. These relations include several bilateral partnerships, dating back, in part, to the origins of the two North American states as European colonies. These bilateral relationships have not always converged or complemented one another; indeed, some have diverged sharply from the pattern seen in others. The key players on the European side of the Atlantic are Britain, France and Germany, whose bilateral relations with the United States and, in the case of Britain and France, also with Canada, have long histories, which are crucial to an understanding of the specific bilateral relationships in existence today. Other European states which are part of NATO and thus of what has often been called the 'Atlantic Community'[1] also form part of the picture.

More broadly, transatlantic relations comprise multilateral relations, and the policies and ideas shared by groups within more than merely two states. Transatlantic relations are thus a many-layered phenomenon. The North Atlantic Treaty (NAT) itself is in part an *ad hoc* common response to external events. Yet it would hardly have survived the demise of its main enemy, communism, and of the communist power base, the Soviet Union, and the dispersal of the Soviet massive military machinery including heavily armed allies, if the Treaty had not been built on internal forces driving the countries on both sides of the Atlantic to follow certain convergent ideals and policies.

To understand transatlantic relations in their complexity, we need to identify the different layers and the factors which distinguish them from, say, the relationship between the United States and Canada on the one hand and Japan on the other, or the relationship between France, Spain and Italy on the one side, and the North African countries on the other. The paper will thus focus on the historical circumstances but also the values and ideals that formed transatlantic relations, on the interest in protecting and promoting them, and on the policies and historical developments that flowed from them.

First, we need to reflect on the ideals which from its creation have inspired the key country in transatlantic relations, the United States of America, and on the way they have come to be shared by the European powers and Canada over time. America's ideals of freedom and democracy, and its aversion to tariffs imposed by its trading partners, date from the declaration of independence. But in the history of the United States, governments have swung between two policies. One attempted to preserve these ideals by protecting their limited power base in the United States itself – limited, compared with the large parts of the globe which did not share these ideals. This policy was pursued either through American isolation from these other parts of the world or through what outsiders would see as the promotion of predominantly 'selfish' economic interests. On the other hand was the policy of using US power to export these ideals to the rest of the world, so that they could gradually come to be applied universally.

For the achievement of either policy – the protection of US ideals and the promotion of these ideals abroad – the United States has always needed and will continue to need partners. In the first instance, these can be powers which through their own actions and policies indirectly protect the United States, in which case no ideological community of values is needed but merely a limited coincidence of interests. In the second instance, America's partners must share its values, perhaps even its missionary zeal. Notwithstanding the halting embrace by post-1815 France of republican ideals, it is only over the last century and a half that the Europeans have grown into established democracies which could be dependable partners for the United States in its universalist policies.

In the light of this consideration, what can we discern about the future functions and possibilities of transatlantic relations? Will cooperation in future be ideals-based (as in the Cold War) or will it rest on the much more fragile basis of *ad hoc* coincidences of political interest, which can turn overnight into bitter economic rivalry?

This takes us to a more tangible level of relations, trade. What makes the trade relationship between Europe and North America more 'special' than that between North America and the Far East is the high level of US investment in Europe and of European investment in North America, and the similarity of the economic structures on both sides of the Atlantic. Moreover, many Europeans share with Americans the belief in the virtues of free trade and in the benefits of a common market. While all three North American countries, like the Europeans, have their 'sacred cows' in domestic industry which they seek to protect, both the single market of the EU and the free trade area in North America prove that there is also great faith in the mutually beneficial effects of the elimination of tariffs and non-tariff barriers. This faith is not shared by several Far Eastern industrialized states which show great reluctance to open their domestic markets to foreign imports on the same scale as they export to the rest of the world.

But there is another level of transatlantic linkage which has little to do with politics, security or economics. It concerns kinship and culture generally. Here we must reflect on the effects of long-term transformations of North American and European societies following changing patterns of immigration and the maturation of independent US and Canadian cultures, which are now more than merely the 'offspring of Europe'.

It is the interaction of factors on these different levels – the ideals-based with its political and security-related consequences, the economic, and the cultural-affective – with developments in the world at large that will determine the future of transatlantic relations.

Chapter 2 of this study will start by looking at the history of the US-European relationships, and the clash and convergence of ideas, until the Second World War. It will then focus on the Atlantic Alliance during the Cold War, trying to cull from history some factors which are likely to remain with us despite the changes taking place on so many levels. The different relationships of the United States with Britain, France, and Germany respectively will be sketched.

Chapter 3 examines a different element in transatlantic relations, Canada, which has very particular relations with the United States on the one hand and with Europe, particularly Britain, on the other.

Chapter 4 gives a *tour d'horizon* of the security context of the 1990s and beyond. Some of the security problems have been with us for a long time, but are now presenting themselves in a new, or more acute, guise. Others are fairly new. Threats to the security of citizens within the North Atlantic Treaty area arise both from outside the countries concerned and from within. The patterns of international action are traced, including the reform of the Atlantic Alliance, formed for the Cold War, to cope with new tasks.

Chapter 5 examines the rise to predominance of economics as the driving force in interstate relations. New economic challenges and the grave problems engendered by the enduring recession and high unemployment are dictating the agendas of governments on both sides of the Atlantic. Most of these problems, as we shall see, affect not only the North Atlantic nations,* but most of the rest of the world.

Chapter 6 explains in greater detail the conceptual problems that have bedevilled transatlantic relations immediately after the Cold War's end. It shows how some European leaders have conceived of the retention of strong transatlantic links as an alternative to further European integration, and why they believed that the loosening of the bonds between the United States and Europe was inevitable. This view is not shared by all European leaders, however, let alone by North Americans.

Chapter 7 will briefly review the proposals which have been put forward since the end of the Cold War for the improvement of transatlantic relations, and for a joint approach to common problems on a regional and global scale. The study concludes by trying to gauge the balance between what will remain of the essence of transatlantic relations and what has changed permanently or will change in the foreseeable future.

---

*This term will be used throughout the text to refer to the members of NATO and/or the USA, Canada and the EU.

Chapter 2

Transatlantic relations in the past

> American policy has always reflected the contest between a universalizing idealism connected with the Puritan origins of the nation, as the secular realization of God's kingdom, and a related desire to withdraw from a corrupted and corrupting world, into the security of national self-sufficiency on an isolated continent.[1]

This is how one American journalist has succinctly summarized the great dialectic of American history, divided between the opposing forces of isolationism and the urge to ensure a universal application of the American ideals. One could develop this dialectic further. The reason why the young United States retreated into isolationism despite its universalizing idealism was that its power base was too slender compared with all those powers throughout the world which did not share its ideals and values. Parallels exist with Robespierre's reluctance to force the values of the French Revolution upon other countries, and with Lenin's decision to content himself with socialism in one country.

US values have a slim chance of survival in the hostile worlds beyond the oceans shielding the continent. What Americans value will only be safe from any threat when it has come to be shared by the whole world: until then, in order to protect these values and the ideals they strive for, US governments must protect their country, the incarnation, the bastion of these values and ideals. If a choice has to be made, America has to come first. Isolation was the answer of the first century of US history. When entangling trade links rendered isolation impossible, US interest, and hence policy, had to try to remove the roots of the threat to its values, that is, to eliminate antagonistic ideologies, whether National-Socialist or communist. But this could not be done at the risk of weakening and

5

destroying the United States itself. For this would mean the destruction of the homebase of American ideals, of 'the American way of life'. And for this, 'as in the Declaration of Independence,' as one key American policy document put it in 1950, '"with a firm reliance on the protection of Divine Providence, we mutually pledge to each other our lives, our Fortunes and our sacred Honor".'[2]

The universalist mission (imposed on the United States by opposition to its political and economic ideals in other continents) has thus been tempered: even with the most powerful economy in the world in the twentieth century, the US has not been and is not able through economic aid and investment to persuade all other countries of the world to adopt its commercial patterns, ideals and values, through defence and economic aid. Thus when it became clear that isolationism was no longer an option,[3] US foreign policy has been aimed at increasing its power through forming coalitions. While there has been a clear preference for alliances with countries which had come to share their ideals and values, US governments on occasion had to compromise, cooperating with non-democratic states so as to offset the main powers inimical to their country. On other occasions, in other contexts, US governments felt compelled to put their narrow national needs above those of even close allies, so as to protect the health of America's economic power base. This interplay between universalism and self-protection is the main dialectic of US policies, and will be seen to run through the present analysis. To outsiders, and particularly to Europeans, the two poles could look either like altruism vs. national selfishness, or like imperialism vs. isolationism. These different possible interpretations of US foreign policy are crucial to the different attitudes of individual European governments to the United States.

Within the pursuit of the American interest, as defined above, Henry Kissinger identified another dialectic. He saw US foreign policy as being driven successively by two opposite ways of thinking: that of President Theodore Roosevelt and that of President Woodrow Wilson. To Kissinger, Theodore Roosevelt 'commands a unique … position in America's approach to international relations', importing ideas and values governing European diplomacy in the nineteenth century into US policy-making, including colonialism and the belief that 'Darwin's theory of the survival of the fittest was a better guide to history than personal morality'.[4] One might interpret Theodore Roosevelt's political principles as a particular fusion between messianic, universalist ambitions (of exporting US ideals) and extreme self-protectionism or national egoism. Kissinger thinks that Theodore Roosevelt's approach to interstate relations 'died with him in 1919, no school of American thought on foreign policy has invoked him since'.[5] Nevertheless, the 'Realist' interpretation of international relations seems to hold many beliefs in common with Roosevelt's approach.

Yet the public rhetoric designed to rally support for US foreign policy is mainly shaped by the spirit of Woodrow Wilson, who symbolized the particular values that the Americans had espoused since the days of Washington and Jefferson. He was the first to apply them to US foreign policies, including policies towards Europe. He is the incarnation of the universalist aspirations of the United States, seeking to reshape the world (or at least Europe) according to US ideals. Wilson shaped American beliefs about how interstate relations should be conducted, effectively until the present day. As Kissinger correctly notes, Wilsonian idealism, his universalism, not the policies of Roosevelt that concentrated primarily on the protection and expansion of the US power base, have since become the keynote of US foreign policy, claiming leadership for the United States on account of its altruism and its unselfish policies: 'from Woodrow Wilson through George Bush, American presidents have invoked their country's unselfishness as the crucial attribute of its leadership role'.[6] And while the reality of US policies might, to a critical observer, contain multiple elements of a more selfish 'national interest', since Wilson's day it has been unacceptable for US governments openly to come to arrangements with other powers that are explicitly built on the rationale of spheres of influence. Yalta is a myth.[7] Wilson's thinking, and that of his successors, was a universalism tempered only by the external obstacles to the export of America's beliefs throughout the world.

Whereas in the first 150 years of its existence America's manifest destiny was pursued in isolation from Europe, since Wilson, and particularly since the Second World War, the United States has perceived its national interest in terms of a universalist aspiration to recreate the world in its own image. Its friends and allies are nations which share the values on which this universalism is founded. Its adversaries are those who seek to destroy them. This can be best understood by scanning the history of relations between the United States and key European countries.

From the American Revolution until the First World War

'The fundamental purpose of the United States is laid down in the Preamble of the Constitution: "… to form a more perfect Union, establish Justice, insure domestic Tranquillity, provide for the common defence, promote the general Welfare, and secure the Blessings of Liberty to ourselves and to our Posterity". In essence, the fundamental purpose is to assure the integrity and vitality of our free society, which is founded upon the dignity and worth of the individual'.[8]

The enduring heritage of the prehistory of the United States is its rejection of the constraints (economic, social and very importantly also religious) of the old feudal and semi-feudal societies of Europe. From the founding myths of the Pilgrim Fathers to the American Revolution of 1774–6, US identity is defined as against that of Europe, and especially of Britain.[9] Together with the economic hardships which forced other Europeans to flee their home country, the political and religious causes of immigration from the United Kingdom became guiding stars of the future United States: the search for religious tolerance, political freedom, social equality and the chance for self-made prosperity, the belief in the virtues of unconstrained economic opportunities, through which the street sweeper could rise to become a millionaire, and through which the British colony could rise to become a world power.

From 1776 to the late nineteenth century

The American Revolution was a revolution against the corrupt *anciens régimes* of the Old World. Part of the Euro-American revolutionary movement, the 'Transatlantic Revolution' of the late eighteenth century, the American Revolution was the sister of the French Revolution. Both French and American ideals of democracy, freedom and equality sprang from European philosophy,[10] as did monarchy, feudalism and all the beliefs revolving around autocratic rule in a centralized, sovereign state.[11] In the American perception, however, democracy, freedom and equality became merged with the Pilgrim Fathers' rejection of the Old World. This anti-European reaction was reinforced by the plight which drove thousands of Europeans annually to choose the uncertainties of a new life in the New World over certain misery in the Old.

The American myth was created, the myth that American values in themselves constituted a rejection of European society as a whole (and not just of some specific clusters and forms of European values). Even

Americans who have the intellectual honesty to admit the European roots of American political philosophy are tempted to contrast American and European values as though they were two distinct belief-systems. Yet in reality, it was the *common* ideals of the French and American Revolutions, and the *common* heritage of British and American Puritanism, Nonconformism and liberalism, that lived on both sides of the Atlantic.

Much critical distance is needed, however, to understand the uneven transformation of societies in both continents from monarchies and oligarchies to democracies. The French like to remind others of their republican history and, like British liberals, they point out that the slave trade was abolished in Europe long before it was abolished in America. Europeans delight in interpreting US policies in terms of national self-interest, hard-nosed political 'Realism' and ruthless power politics. Americans, by contrast, note the relapses of France into the assorted empires and monarchies which succeeded unstable republics in rapid sequence. They frown at the persistence of the institutionalized inequality among the citizens of Britain, the Netherlands, Sweden and Spain, where monarchs and nobility continue to play their quaint but unrepublican roles in society. And they point to the monsters of fascism and Stalinism to which Europe gave birth in the twentieth century.

This has led to strange mutual misunderstandings. The Americans tend to see themselves and their country as the beacon of liberty in the world, their foreign policy as one that brings this light to all the corners of the earth. Europeans, particularly the French, have their own democratic and humanitarian tradition to be proud of. Each side points to the beam in the other's eye, neither acknowledging that in its own.

From the late nineteenth century until 1917
Towards the end of the nineteenth century, the Americans ventured forth from the splendid isolation of their continent, affected by the spread of imperialism from across the Atlantic, which blended in well with the missionary zeal of the messianism which they had shown in their conquest of territory on their own continent. From isolationist protectionism of its ideals, America embarked on its first attempt to export those ideals for the benefit of other parts of the world. Theodore Roosevelt's colonialism, directed at Cuba, Puerto Rico and the Philippines, could be portrayed by his more idealistic countrymen as liberation from the yoke of corrupt, Old-Worldly Spanish imperialism. European imperialism bad; American imperialism liberation: this was the simplistic conviction that provided the first stepping stone between US isolation and engagement in world affairs.

While most Europeans continued to be the United States' chief adversaries (as both imperialist rivals and political antitheses), Britain, America's existential antithesis, managed to win Washington's favour. They built on the period of mutual tolerance which had developed from the deterrent formulations of the Monroe Doctrine of 1823, in which the US president of that name urged the British to keep to their part of the world if they did not want further trouble with their self-confident ex-colonies. The British turned this to their advantage by regarding it as a promise that they need not expect trouble from the other side of the Atlantic, as long as they themselves played by the rules formulated by Monroe. With their backs free in this way, they could concentrate on other parts of their empire; this worked greatly to their advantage.

From this unideological symbiosis there developed at the end of the nineteenth century a very un-Wilsonian, Theodore Rooseveltian rapprochement, driven in a good part by Anglo-Saxon tribal instincts and by shared economic beliefs (hard-nosed capitalism and free trade) rather than by any shared democratic ideals. The flirtations between the leaders of the British Empire and the advocates of a US imperial mission at the end of the nineteenth century and the beginning of the twentieth did much to infect America with the sins of the Old World, rather than guiding the Old World towards the values of democracy and equality.

While this rapprochement certainly helped to lay the foundations of what would eventually become the British–US 'special relationship', the convergence of US and British policies was not wholly innocent in terms of America's earlier revolutionary and later Wilsonian self-perception. If the United States stands by its own values of democracy and (racial) equality, it can logically entertain especially good relations with any country upholding the same values. It is then hard pressed, however, to explain an especially close relationship with a country which, if judged by the supreme contemporary Western criteria of what constitutes a democracy (namely, degree of enfranchisement of the population and freedom of elections) was essentially undemocratic before the First World War: until the Representation of the People Act of 1918, only 30% of the British population of 20 years and over could vote in general elections.[12] As we shall see, there were more conceptual problems with such an exceptionally close relationship even after 1928, when Britain became a full democracy. By then, and even more after 1945, many equally democratic nations vied for America's attention.

Encounters of ideas: 1917–19

When the United States was finally dragged into yet another undemocratic war among the imperialist dinosaurs of the Old World in 1917, President Wilson presented the strength of democratic ideals to explain the righteousness of US involvement. Under him, the United States fought for democracy, self-determination and free trade. Under the momentum of US political and propaganda leadership, the French and the British were forced to confront the logical clash between their self-image as liberal democracies and the dubious moral legitimacy of their empires. Freedom for their colonized peoples was dictated to the defeated empires of the Great War. The victorious powers, Britain and France, reluctantly had to agree under US pressure to a long-term programme of decolonization, via the interim stage of the mandate system. The rhetoric of freedom from colonial rule (addressed to the peoples ruled by the rival powers), which Britain and France had adopted during the war under the influence of their own liberals and of US idealism, now came to haunt them. The promise of self-rule for the Arabs and the peoples of Eastern Europe went hand in hand with a promise of eventual self-determination for all peoples worldwide, as postulated by Wilson himself. Much against the wishes of the more conservative and less democratic forces, strong in both countries, Britain and France were pushed into subscribing to these European-American ideals whether in word or in – hesitant – action.

Crucial here is the difference between two definitions of 'nationalism'. As in the purest French republican tradition (which, alas, has not always dominated French politics since the Revolution), the US concept of nationhood is not an ethnic one, but an integrative, civic idea. The emphasis on the nation in the US is not directed against anybody, but aimed to unite US citizens of different backgrounds and different races to support common ideals and common values. Wilson crucially failed to understand European *ethnic* nationalism, and unwittingly gave it ample leverage by insisting on the right of collective national self-determination as a basic principle for the world order he helped to create in Paris. The Europeans perverted this into a blank cheque for ethnic fission: to this day ever smaller ethnic groups claim the right to self-determination, to independent statehood, and to the suppression of even smaller minorities within the territory they claim for themselves.

For European nationalism in the nineteenth century had increasingly acquired ugly ethnic criteria, the logic of which inescapably led to the intolerance of ethnic minorities within the body of the ethnic 'nation'.

The step towards the atrocities committed by *National*-Socialist Germany (or indeed the 'ethnic cleansing' in Yugoslavia in the early 1990s) was a logical one, though fortunately not taken throughout Europe. Nevertheless, ethnic overtones to European nationalism remain to this day, and are among the most crucial factors dividing Americans and Europeans. It can be demonstrated that subsequent transatlantic cooperation was only possible with Europeans who consciously turned away from such an ethnic logic.

The trauma of isolationism and the lessons of the Second World War

Ideals born in Europe, applied in America, rekindled or strengthened in Europe through the influence of Wilsonianism at the end of the First World War, thus introduced into international politics a new universalist, missionary element. The new world order which was created was based on these ideals. Formally, it found its expression in the League of Nations, on faith in human reason and enlightened understanding of the connections between an individual's own interests and those of his or her neighbours. But form and faith lacked force.

Without the underpinning of punitive force, the ideal failed to become reality. What became reality instead was the domination of the world by nationalist selfishness of an even more vicious form than the nineteenth century, the cursed mother of nationalism, had witnessed. The United States, at once the strongest and the most idealistic nation, thought that it could afford to retreat once again from the world. But this retreat contributed to the failure of US ideals and the new world order Wilson had sought to create. It spelled doom for Europe, and defeat for the kindred spirits the United States had found in Europe. France, Britain, Belgium, the Netherlands, in short the countries which by now shared US ideals, were too weak to face the dictators alone. Without being able to build on the reassurance of a commitment by the United States, they were all at some stage forced into tolerance of the intolerable, into appeasement, and in some cases into occupation and collaboration.

Meanwhile the United States stood by – until in 1941 Japan attacked Pearl Harbor and Hitler declared war on the US. The shock for Americans was such that, despite some Midwestern rhetoric, they have never again felt able to insulate themselves against the ravages of major wars occurring in other parts of the globe. Moreover, it has engendered in many Americans the belief that 'European stability is vital to our own security, a lesson we have learned twice at great cost this century'.[13]

Sorting out Europe (again): 1941–47

Brought for a second time in less than 25 years into a major war in Europe against their wishes, Americans began to give particular attention to the role of Europe in their own foreign relations. They began to realize that Europe itself was and continued to be torn apart by its own contradictory philosophies and values, and that the United States shared the position of one of these two sides. Europe was in fact the battleground of the European-US universalist beliefs in freedom, liberal democracy, free market economies on the one hand, and on the other European products such as ethnic nationalism, one-party states, police-states, centrally planned economies, government control of information, and great-power domination.

But the faultlines ran not only through the anti-Axis alliance – where the US found itself fighting alongside the Stalinist USSR – but also through individual European countries themselves. During the war, France relapsed into authoritarian autocracy (and collaboration coupled with racist persecutions) under Marshal Pétain. Britain, under Churchill's otherwise admirable statesmanship, relapsed into its imperialist proclivity for great-power spheres of influence.[14] Meanwhile it was the Americans, under Franklin D. Roosevelt's universalist idealism, who insisted that the Yalta agreement should require free elections to be held throughout the areas liberated from German and Italian rule.

Even after the end of the war against Hitler and Mussolini, when they discovered the Soviet hydra lurking behind the defeated monsters of Germany and Italy, the British did not worry so much about Stalin's ideology, his domestic policies, his totalitarian rule of terror. Instead, they worried about the Soviet threat to British colonial interests – Iran, the Mediterranean, the British route to India and beyond – in much the same way as they had worried before about the Tsar marching into India. It was thus not the British but the Americans who, alerted by the British to the expansionist pattern underlying Soviet behaviour, began to recognize Stalinist communism as fundamentally antagonistic to the US ideals of democracy, freedom and the individual's right to prosperity. Finally persuaded that they would not remain unmolested if another rival ideology extended its power base throughout the world, the Americans began to see this rivalry in terms of a universal contest which could be resolved only through the ultimate triumph of one ideology over the other.

One might venture the guess that even without the Cold War, American leaders by now would have regarded it as largely in their interest that their shared ideals should come into flower and predominate in Europe, this economically and strategically crucial part of the world. It was seen as generally in America's interest that as much of the world as possible should share its beliefs in democracy and the free market. Europe was at once the first line of the defence of American values, and an ally or even springboard for spreading them further. In the words of the US defence expert Catherine Kelleher, 'The existence of a Europe "like us" was a precondition to the establishment of an international order conducive to American political and economic interests.'[15]

Moreover, even before a communist threat was recognized, the United States had essentially abandoned the isolationist option. Instead, it joined a new permanent system to secure a new world order: the United Nations. Like the League of Nations before it, its design was strongly influenced by US ideals. But this time it was to have US backing. US membership here (where it had been absent in the League) meant a commitment to the export and universal application of America's ideals. Thus the US went from isolationism to universalism. In this context, the country's leaders saw their UN Security Council partners Britain and France, countries which had come to share the same values, as chief allies (and thus force-multipliers) in this universal battle for the democratic Euro-American values enshrined in the UN Charter.

The Cold War alliance

> Three realities emerge as a consequence of [the] purpose [of the
> United States]: Our determination to maintain the essential elements
> of individual freedom, as set forth in the Constitution and Bill of
> Rights; our determination to create conditions under which our free
> democratic system can live and prosper; and our determination to
> fight if necessary to defend our way of life...[16]

By 1947, the conditions under which the American free democratic system could live and prosper had begun to be seen as endangered directly by the Soviet Union.

America takes the lead: 1947–90

Stalin's Soviet Union had shown its expansionist tendencies by bringing all of Eastern Europe (except Greece) under its sway during or immediately after the Second World War. Coupled with this process was an ideology that fanned the flames of civil war in Greece, sparked off anticolonial insurrections throughout Asia and, subsequently, other parts of the world, and endangered the fragile republics of France and Italy. 'The ultimate objective of Soviet-directed world communism is the domination of the world,' it was asserted in a key US government policy document of 1948.[17] This challenge was strong enough to unite most of the West European and North Atlantic powers.

This time, rather than waiting for an enemy to come to it, the United States decided to contain this new opponent, indeed defeat it through action short of war. The US objective became 'to reduce the power and influence of Moscow to limits where they will no longer constitute a threat to the peace and stability of international society', and 'to bring about a basic change in the theory and practice of international relations observed by the government in power in Russia'.[18] As Russia was endangering international security, it had to be made to change and accept US principles, at least in foreign relations.

America's first line of defence was wherever the opponent sought to increase its power or the territory it controlled. Europe seemed particularly threatened: the Baltic states could not be rescued; Poland, Hungary, Bulgaria and Romania fell from Nazi oppression to Soviet tyranny; Greece was burning; Czechoslovakia fell; and Italy and France seemed in danger of going the same way. Recent experiences of comradeship in arms, ties of kinship, the common values shared with the democracies in Europe helped the United States to break with its isolationist traditions. George Washington's admonition never to be caught in entangling alliances was cast aside to create the North Atlantic alliance.

Western Europe (or 'Free Europe') as a whole was seen both as a potential victim of communist ideological or military expansion, and also as an ally for the United States, if only its economies, its faith in democracy, and its armed forces could be strengthened to enable it to hold out by itself against Soviet ideological and military pressure. US leaders did not anticipate how much European security would cost them in terms of military commitment, economic aid, political attention and diplomatic wrangling.

But even at this cost, North Americans and Europeans shared the conviction that this time, unlike in the two world wars, a great conflagration might be avoided through a show of solidarity and resolve *vis-à-vis* the Soviet Union. US policy-makers from Kennan to Bush hoped to achieve the defeat of Soviet communism through means other than hot war. And if this could be achieved, a fairly large price seemed worth paying in terms of military aid, deployment of nuclear weapons and military personnel, and economic aid.

It also seemed worthwhile backing the West Europeans on most issues, at least where they were not totally at odds with America's anti-colonial ideals of freedom and universal self-determination. The Europeans had an exasperating tendency to relapse into their bad old colonial ways, or to play balance-of-power games of national rivalry with one another which only the United States could sort out. But if this was what was needed to keep the Red Army at bay and Soviet missiles in their silos, then the United States would spend the time, money and energy to do so.

And in the process, US leaders experienced again what they had first tasted during the two world wars: the feeling of power. Ultimately, leadership, indeed world leadership, fell in easily with America's sense of itself as a morally superior society; yet Americans liked to see themselves as a world power against their will. In their commitment to their own values, now codified in the Charter of the United Nations, they could hardly again reject the role of enforcer of these values. Therefore, whether in Europe or elsewhere, Americans now had to play a leading role. This was a new experience, carrying the temptation to start playing the sort of power politics which they had so long condemned in Europeans – even though American leaders would not have admitted to this in public rhetoric. Throughout the Cold War, and no less today, the balance between resentment of the cost and the welcoming of influence has shifted, but neither has ever been or will ever be completely absent.

Alliance friction and cooperation

There was a basic consensus among the twelve countries which signed the North Atlantic Treaty in April 1949:[19] any further spread of communism had to be prevented. Nevertheless, some differing national priorities, interpretations of the most useful action in certain critical situations, remained and were structurally unavoidable. Differing analyses of the international situation (and of national budgetary requirements) continued to be made by each government separately.

From the time when the treaty was first negotiated secretly between the United States, Britain and Canada in spring 1948 until the outbreak of the Korean war, it was generally thought that the communist threat was mainly political. But the invasion of South Korea by the North in June 1950 convinced the North Atlantic nations that a new aspect of the danger had now come to the fore, namely the military aspect. All agreed on the need to create an integrated military structure and a planning organization to complement the treaty: in short, the Organization of the North Atlantic Treaty. All agreed on the need to strengthen their defences, build up their armed forces, and try to deter a Soviet attack on Western or Southern Europe.

But disagreements between European governments and the successive administrations soon began. For the victims of repeated German aggression it was difficult to swallow German rearmament, however sensible it would have been to add 500,000 West German soldiers to NATO's strength. Supported by US President Eisenhower, Greece and Turkey wanted to become NATO members; but the British would have preferred to see Turkey in a Middle East defence organization, yet to be created. From the early 1950s, France, and soon also Britain, had reservations about the aggressiveness with which the United States had pursued (since 1948) its subversive policies against communist regimes. Different policies towards Mao's regime soon emerged, leading to recognition of communist China by Britain in 1949, by France in 1964 and only in 1972 by the United States.

In particular, US policies towards European colonies or protectorates tended to differ decisively from those of Britain, France, the Netherlands, Belgium, Portugal and other European colonial powers which felt that they were fighting communists via anti-colonial forces; Washington, however, thought it would be playing into the hands of the communists to oppose independence movements.

Paris and London were particularly at odds with Washington over their assessment of how communist-supported nationalism should be handled in North Africa in the 1950s. The US pressure which cut short the Anglo-French Suez campaign was the tip of the iceberg in this respect.

The French felt insufficiently supported by the Americans in Indochina in the early 1950s; indeed they felt betrayed, for as soon as they withdrew from Southeast Asia the Americans took their place. This largely explains France's hostility towards the US position during the Vietnam war throughout the 1960s. But there was little understanding for Washington's policies on this issue anywhere in Europe in the 1960s and 1970s.

Moreover, differences about how free Europe might be defended and about how the Soviets should be dealt with were very pronounced during the Cold War. Even from the early 1950s they focused on different preferences with regard to nuclear strategy. The Europeans were horrified when President Truman at a press conference in late 1950 talked of using nuclear weapons in the context of the Korean war. While initially (and before the Soviet development of intercontinental missiles) the Americans seemed too trigger-happy for the Europeans, from the late 1950s onwards Europeans were distressed about the US preference for a conventional defence of Europe, where they would have preferred early use of nuclear weapons to shock the Soviets into ending a war. This

17

difference persisted until the end of the Cold War; it was a factor in France's departure from the integrated military structure of NATO, and also in determined efforts among the remaining NATO members to paper over the deep cracks and to bank on deterrence through solidarity, rather than through a truly credible, agreed strategy.

Despite this effort to achieve solidarity (which enabled NATO to adopt its last Cold War doctrine, MC 14/3, in 1967), the cracks remained. They were deepened by repeated American initiatives aimed at reducing US force strengths in Europe and at encouraging Europeans to increase their manpower.

The gradually evolving US tendency to liaise with the Soviets bilaterally, over the heads of the Europeans, gave rise to and nurtured the myth that a deal might be made about the fate of Europe. The very limited consultation with Europeans before the conclusion of US–Soviet arms control deals in the 1970s and again in the late 1980s (despite European dependency on America's nuclear shield) led to much misunderstanding.

Structurally, transatlantic relations were also made problematic by the instability of the US governmental system, with its lack of continuity in personnel and its susceptibility to major swings. While European governments tended to be quite flexible in negotiations with one another and with Washington, as long as they could keep issues away from public debate, almost all issues (from doctrine to force deployment to negotiations with the USSR) tended to become subjects for in-fighting within the American administration or, worse still, between the administration and Congress. This then tended to tie the hands of US negotiators, making it more difficult for them to come to a compromise agreement than it was for many of their European colleagues.

Nevertheless, one important lesson of the 1967–90 period is that, notwithstanding this structural impediment in the US government, it was perfectly possible for the Europeans to have their interests taken into account within NATO. Britain and the Federal Republic of Germany, in particular, discovered that by concerting their positions in advance, they could have a persuasive influence on US negotiators.[20] Even smaller powers, such as the Netherlands or Spain, not to mention powers in particular strategic positions such as Norway or Turkey, found that they were listened to on many occasions.

NATO was thus impressively successful, deterring aggression in the Treaty area, despite the fragility of its transatlantic consensus on defence doctrine, and despite the many structural impediments which bedevilled this voluntary alliance among quarrelsome, largely selfish states. Crucially, however, the collective self-interest of these states which often remembered their shared values only in their common rhetoric was driven into convergence by consistent outside pressure from the Soviet Union and its satellites. These usually convinced the 16 members[21] of the alliance of the need for consensus on major measures. NATO supporters to this day favour this procedure of forging agreement; it is important to remember, however, what a crucial role the shared perception of a threat against all members played in the process; also the crucial role of the US as consensus builder, because it was and is by far the most powerful among the allies.

While the above describes relations among NATO allies in general, transatlantic relations from the time of the American Revolution to the present have comprised aspects specific to individual countries. Britain, France and Germany, also Italy and, in another way, Sweden, all see themselves as having a special relationship with the United States, even though the term is most commonly associated with Britain.

British–US relations

Although the United Kingdom was the chief enemy and focus of negative self-identification during and for some years after America's revolutionary decoupling from Europe, many Britons continue to see Americans as part of their own wider family. The wave of thinking in terms of race and ethnic kinship that swept through Europe towards the end of the nineteenth and the beginning of the twentieth centuries led Britons to think extremely kindly about Americans, Britain's favourite allies by far.[22]

The comradeship in arms with the Americans experienced during both world wars made the British feel it was easy to do business (on all levels) with people who – despite their idealism and great generosity – were pragmatic and got to the point. For a variety of other reasons, not least their noted reluctance to learn foreign languages, the English in particular enjoyed working with Americans (and Canadians, Australians and New Zealanders) more than with most of their European neighbours.

The handover of power from John Bull to Uncle Sam, a process under way from the Second World War until the 1960s, was strangely acceptable to Britain: Britons responded with a striking absence of resentment. Much has been written on this subject, and many purely rational explanations have been attempted.[23] But it is difficult to rid oneself of the impression that deeply irrational forces were at work in numbing Britain's pain while its empire was being amputated limb by limb. Britons seemed oddly insensitive to what was really happening, namely, that America was taking Britain's and France's place in most parts of the world, and that the two European countries were being reduced, both consequently and incidentally, to second-rate powers. While there were anti-American sentiments, particularly on the far right and the far left of the British electoral spectrum, for example in the wake of the Suez affair, they are insignificant in comparison with French feelings about the US.

There are explanations for this. One is that the British developed and retained with the United States and Canada a special and exclusive intelligence-sharing relationship which has survived both the Second World War and the Cold War. Another is that the United States made Britain, as the world's third nuclear power,[24] an exception to the general rule whereby it refused to share nuclear technology.[25] But these two reasons together still only go a short way to explain the feeling the majority of Britons have for America. The affection which exists on the British side goes much deeper and is much less rational. It is rooted in language and culture, also perhaps in a certain fondness many Britons feel for an 'alternative' Anglo-Saxon culture, in which they can easily find their way around, and where conventions seem more relaxed and human relations simpler, and there is much less of the reserve Britons both treasure and suffer from.

On a cultural level, the majority culture in America, from Christmas carols to Humpty Dumpty, from the pseudo-Oxbridge architecture of Yale and Princeton to Georgian neoclassicism (now held to be an indigenous form of American architecture), is British in origin. British feelings towards Americans are largely reciprocated, as opinion polls in the US conducted in 1994 show: Britons rank only after Canadians on the 'sympathy thermometer' measuring US affections for other countries.[26]

Crucially, despite some linguistic modification which English has undergone in American mouths, there is still some admiration for British English and for the clarity with which British officials usually write their own language. Perhaps this is why British diplomats and military men come away from discussions with the impression that they have been listened to and that they have influenced – decisively influenced – the Americans. Indeed, British officials have long prided themselves on being, in the words of Prime Minister Harold Macmillan, the wise Greeks guiding the 'great big, vulgar, bustling' Roman-Americans, or on being the pragmatic, even machiavellian politicians who bring the idealistic and naive Americans to their senses.[27]

To what extent any of this is true is quite unfathomable. It may well be that the highly skilled draftsmanship of British officials and their (unsurprisingly) better command of their native language compared with other NATO allies or UN members has frequently led to the adoption of British draft proposals as texts for international statements. But American officials tend on the whole to react dismissively or even with some hostility to questions about British influence. It seems that they do not cherish the notion that they are being manipulated by the British. But are they? Certainly, the many rival decision-making centres in Washington allow skilful outsiders access to many different points where leverage can be applied. But they may also give people the impression that they have exerted important influence, when in reality they have merely been listened to by one of many key individuals, whose plans may or may not become government policy. Perhaps some British diplomats are truly the *éminences grises* who hold the threads of Washington's (and indeed Atlantic alliance) policy in their hands. Perhaps they just think they are; perhaps Washington manipulates the British to defend its policies in Europe by exploiting their fear of losing what they *believe* to be their special relationship with the United States.

Be that as it may, all these points only go some way towards explaining this extraordinary phenomenon by which a nation, a governing elite, allowed itself to become the appendage of an ascendant power, having been in turn its ancestor and its chief enemy and later rival in international relations. This elite and its nation also studiously avoid facing up to the fact that if the United States is close to Britain today, it is because Britain's political system and hence its ideas have changed fundamentally since 1776, not because the Americans' have. The British understanding of the world is one in which Britain has not changed, ideologies do not matter, and enemies and allies come and go – except for one ally, the United States, to which their fate has been wedded since 1941.[28]

Amazingly, this deliberate blindness on the part of the British goes so far as to deny that they have lost any sovereignty from granting military bases to the United States on British soil, with what *de facto* amounts to total US control over them.[29] While this was necessary for the credibility (through real operability) of NATO's deterrence strategy, it nonetheless meant the concession of a slice of British sovereignty, a concession made by other, but by no means all other, NATO allies. For example, de Gaulle found it unacceptable, as did Denmark and Norway. Much lesser concessions of rights to the European Union, on the other hand, are loudly proclaimed by Britons to be completely unacceptable infringements of their sovereignty. This British schizophrenia with regard to relations with Washington on the one hand and Brussels on the other is often explained in terms of Britain's support for NATO, which ultimately works under intergovernmental control, whereas the first pillar of the European Union, with its qualified majority voting, has the flavour of supranationality, feared greatly by many Britons. Yet the reality of dependence on the United States cannot with the best of all wills be described as intergovernmental alliance among equals. Nevertheless, the UK's different attitudes towards Washington and the EU will in all likelihood remain.

Moreover, the 'special relationship' has played an important role (next to the existence of the Commonwealth) in persuading Britain of its distinctiveness from the rest of Europe. Despite contrary intentions on the part of US administrations from Eisenhower's to Kennedy's, American closeness to Britain (added to Britain's Commonwealth ties) hardened London's determination not to join in European integration in the 1950s. Once admitted into the EEC, belatedly, in 1973, Britain continued to stall on any European measures that could possibly be interpreted as aimed at greater independence from the United States. British government circles remain apparently unaffected by individual well-placed Americans who encourage them at regular intervals to play a more positive role in Europe, as US interest in Britain is proportionate to Britain's influence in the EU. But as Raymond Seitz, US ambassador to London under the Bush administration, noted:

> Embedded in this view ... is a contradiction. While America strongly supports the concept of European integration, we at the same time are anxious that Britain preserve its capacity for independent action, within Europe and beyond the continent as well. In the strictest sense, this is a military question – that ... Britain retain more than an irreducible minimum of defense capability which enables it to affect events and to act on a broad stage.[30]

It is not surprising that, couched in these terms, the message received in London consistently reads: be our partner in a special, global relation-ship![31] Declared dead many times,[32] the 'special relationship' between Britain and the US is unlikely to disappear while the two peoples speak the same language, and while both of them wish for a more limited integration of Europe than many European powers.

Franco-US relations

The key paradox of European–US relations centres on the Franco-American relationship. Its love-hatred, its sibling rivalry, its competitiveness are at the heart of any divergences today between European and US interests, and are crucial to this study. France and the United States, two republics, the two defenders of human rights and democracy, have in the second half of the twentieth century become direct rivals as much as partners. This is not because their values differ: indeed, most of their key values are identical.[33] As President Chirac wrote in February 1996, 'Few nations have been marked by the ideal of universalism as much as ours.' He might have added: this is also true of the United States. In fact he was writing on the eve of his visit there.[34] He told the US Congress that the 'special relationship between the United States and France is founded on a common vision of the world, the same faith in democracy, liberty, human rights, and the state ruled by law'.[35] It is *because* French and US values are so similar that France finds it intolerable to fall meekly into line behind a power that is claiming moral leadership of the world on the strength of these values.

Few Frenchmen have forgiven the United States for what they see as a slight against their civilization. France gave the Americans a good part of their revolutionary philosophy:[36] France was the first country to recognize the young, independent federation.[37] As General André Beaufre put it in 1966, 'We in France assisted at your birth'.[38] Thirty years on, President Chirac told the US Congress 'how much France helped your country to constitute itself as a free, sovereign, independent nation'.[39] French interest in the fate of the US experiment in the nineteenth century thus was more sympathetic than almost any other country's. French people across the political spectrum see their country as a sort of fairy godmother to the United States, which irritatingly refuses to pay it the respect due to it.[40]

Indeed, they acutely resent the fact that American English, not French, is becoming the language of technology and communication worldwide; one need only think of the persistence with which French officials use French, not English, at international conferences. French governments and industry are trying to fight the pervasiveness of English to this day.[41] French leaders believe that their country (whose nuclear weapons make it the third most important military power in the world, as presidents since Valéry Giscard d'Estaing have repeatedly reminded us[42]) is as important, in cultural and philosophical if not in military terms, as the United States.

'Our only rival', wrote one Gaullist politician, 'is America'.[43] French attitudes reflect 'the bitterness of a nation which once was in the world's first rank, with regard to a vigorous giant which has snatched away its primacy'.[44] None of this is auspicious for Franco-US relations.

As regards what America has done for France, however, many French people have a more cynical view than the British of US aid to the Entente powers in the First World War and to the Western Allies in the Second. The French often point out that the United States came in very late, too late, in the latter conflict, to save France, and then exacted the prize of military hegemony in NATO.[45] Although Americans joined up in droves in the two wars to defend or liberate France, the country of Lafayette, the French pay little tribute in public rhetoric to the gallantry of the US servicemen who died on French soil. Where American intellectuals in both wars discovered the unsurpassable charms of 'gay Paree', inspiring American popular and elite culture alike, the French mostly reacted as though any American in Paris was a curse more than a source of welcome revenue to an economically exhausted country.

Expecting gratitude for French actions 150 years earlier, but miserly with their own gratitude for American deeds this century, the French were bound for a course of friction with the United States. This is despite the fact that during the early days of the Cold War, French leaders were among those who tried to obtain a US commitment to European security, who pushed for the creation of the Atlantic alliance, and who eagerly offered Paris and the surrounding area to house the chief military and political headquarters of NATO.[46]

But the resulting organization was too Anglo-Saxon for France's liking, and it did not deal with all the issues which were vital to France. Unlike the British, the French saw the Americans as conspiring to replace them in Southeast Asia and the Middle East, and the painful loss of their own colonies in bloody wars made the French less charitably disposed towards those whom they suspected of wanting to usurp their place. By 1958, after de Gaulle had rescued France from an acute political crisis over Algeria, he was ready to confront the United States: he demanded equal treatment, recognition as a world power on equal terms with the United States and Britain, or, he explained to President Eisenhower, France would draw the consequences with regard to NATO membership.[47] By 1965, de Gaulle had become convinced that his conditions would not be met. He decided to announce in 1966 that France would no longer be part of the integrated military structure.

From 1958 onwards, France was the most difficult of the United States'

European allies, always asking for more privileges and more concessions than the Americans were prepared to grant. Despite some steps towards more pragmatic cooperation in the ensuing decades, France continued to be the odd man out in NATO and in transatlantic relations. Franco-American relations were consistently painful on both sides: hurt pride here, profound irritation there, stood as stumbling blocks between the two oldest allies. And between them, there was always the special Anglo-American relationship, a continuous source of jealousy for France, which would have preferred to be in Britain's position.[48] Instead, France was consistently humiliated in the 1950s and early 1960s by exclusion from the Anglo-American *tête-à-tête*.[49]

Crucial also is the US–Gaullist difference in perception of world politics. Where Americans saw their involvement in the international arena in terms of a struggle for ideas of freedom and democracy against any power opposing these, the French after de Gaulle tended to see the world in terms of nation-states, whose differing ideologies were less relevant. While some of de Gaulle's successors went back to pre-Gaullist ideas of European integration, there was no doubt that all of them saw France and America, or Europe and America, as rival powers in a worldwide contest. For de Gaulle, communist Russia, too, was a potential partner in a big balance-of-power game which did not focus on who was ideologically good or bad, but on who could help France offset its rival, the United States.

Even when the Cold War drew to its end, this thinking still dominated French politics. Confident that the end of the Warsaw Pact would entail the disintegration of NATO, the French government put its cards on an alternative European security structure.[50] It was with great surprise that French leaders noted that none of the other countries were prepared to see NATO disappear, and that no one else wanted to see the Americans leave Europe.[51] Thus, though Franco-US relations had never been cordial since 1958, they reached a significant low in the immediate post-Cold War years.[52] Opinion polls show that American sympathy for France in 1994 was only just greater than that for Russia.[53]

But the nadir of Franco-American relations was slowly overcome. Crucial to this were the lessons France drew from the Gulf war: the relative poverty of its own contribution, its dependence on the United States for satellite intelligence, and the much greater effectiveness of the contribution of the UK.[54] France's leaders have come to understand that their European allies are opposed to any purely European defence structure outside NATO; in other words, a European defence identity will be created within NATO or not at all.[55] In particular, the leaders of the Gaullist RPR (Rassemblement pour la République) which has been the senior partner in French governments since 1993, have now come to the conclusion that it is no longer in France's national interest to *faire cavalier seul*, to be the lone horseman going about his business outside the alliance when all the other powers concert their operations. A new era in France's relations with its allies arguably started with the decision announced in December 1995 (but long in the making) to rejoin certain planning committees of NATO, albeit not the integrated military structure. Along with his predecessors since Giscard d'Estaing, President Chirac has unequivocally called 'the political engagement of the United States in Europe and its military presence on the European soil ... an essential factor in the stability and security of the continent, as much as of the world'.[56]

Nevertheless, France is likely to remain a challenging partner for the United States. Even though for several years pragmatism has tempered France's principles,[57] the fundamental considerations guiding French foreign and defence policy will not disappear overnight. Indeed, as will be shown later, the Franco-American rivalry has in 1990–95 been at the crux of the tensions between Europe and the United States which led to some pessimism about transatlantic relations in the first half of this decade.

German–US relations

US relations with Germany are slightly less complex than those with Britain and much less so than those with France. Many Americans had German ancestors at the time of the First and Second World Wars: the largest single group[58] of Americans who answered census inquiries about their ethnic origin claimed descent from Germany (45.6 million or 18.3% of the US population). Many Americans fought the Germans in the two world wars more in sorrow than in anger, and treated them with exceptional kindness after their defeat in 1945. It was commonly known in Germany that to be a prisoner of war under the Americans was preferable to anything else. Towards the end of hostilities, Germans in the areas concerned generally awaited the arrival of US occupying forces eagerly as a liberation from mortal danger, not with the fear of reprisals that was widespread in other parts of Germany. Not having suffered excessively themselves, and not having experienced German occupation, American GIs found it much easier to treat the defeated Germans leniently.

With images of the evil Hun less deeply ingrained in the collective memory, Americans since 1945 have found it easier than Germany's

European neighbours to believe subsequent generations of Germans when they claim that Germany is no longer racist, authoritarian, abominable. The great majority of Americans are descendants of people from other countries and other cultures, who can believe that just as they, as Americans, are different from their European ancestors, the Germans could change to become peace-loving and democratic.

Americans also tend to find German businessmen and politicians reasonably easy to deal with: they speak English without letting national pride get in the way (as tends to be the case with the French), they accept that America's enterprises are larger, and that if Germans want to do business with the US, it is they who have to adapt.

American politicians, officials and military men soon recognized the weight of the Federal Republic in strategic, economic and political terms: this frontline state was particularly important for NATO's defence, not least because its conventional forces provided the bulk of the alliance's forces in Central Europe. Here was a healthy economy that had made the most of Marshall aid, a government which made alignment with the United States the mainstay of security policy. In more than merely military terms, the FRG was the key bastion around which the Americans built the security of NATO during the Cold War. Since its end, and in the absence of a clear representation of Europe on the part of the European Commission, Washington sees Germany as its most important European partner, economically and in many ways politically. Since German reunification, both President Bush and President Clinton have offered Bonn 'partnership in leadership', much to the chagrin of London and Paris.[59] Though less popular than the Canadians and the British, Germans are seen in mainly positive terms by Americans, as recent opinion polls show.[60]

The Germans have been grateful recipients of US trust. Alone untarnished by appeasement, defeat or economic exhaustion, the United States came out of both wars as a potential new idol for the citizens of the Federal Republic. Untarnished also by long histories of fratricidal wars and internecine feuds, America's new society, its idealism, lack of cynicism, and civic notion of nationalism provided guiding lights for West Germany's own social, political, economic and cultural transformation.

The United States, with its generosity, its lack of vindictiveness, became the new model for the Bonn republic it helped to shape. Care parcels, Marshall aid, grants for young Germans to study at US universities, investment and a buzzing, optimistic youth culture from the 1940s until well into the 1960s made the United States the synonym in Germany for prosperity and progress. The kindness of Americans contrasted

27

with the inability of other Europeans to look at the present without the lens of the past. Germans, in the first 25 years after the Second World War, aspired to be the prize pupil in the class of America's European dependants. They were so eager to please Truman, Eisenhower and indeed Kennedy that for a long time they were determined to believe that there could not be differences of interest between them.

It was therefore all the more difficult for the Germans to come to terms with the fallibility of their new model, and disillusionment came on several levels. German governments began to notice from the late 1950s that in NATO Americans preached one thing and did another, and that even the altruistic United States occasionally had its own security more at heart than Germany's. Initially, they simply could not believe what was happening: time and again, they were determined to see differences (over nuclear strategy from 1955, over the handling of Berlin in 1958–62, over *Ostpolitik*) as mere misunderstandings.

But coupled with the proof of US fallibility – both military and ethical – in Southeast Asia, the gradual realization of the differences between them often resulted in unreasonably harsh German criticism of the United States. All too high moral expectations of the Americans at times gave way to all too harsh judgment. For good and bad reasons, left-wing intellectuals, in particular, revelled in anti-US sentiments in the late 1970s and the early 1980s. Again for good and bad reasons, conservative Germans saw the US consumer society, geared towards rapid turnover and superficial enjoyment, as a threat to their own Biedermeier values.

Importantly, also, there was the commitment to European integration, synonym for reconciliation and integration with France and the other West European victims of German aggression in the twentieth century, which often faced German leaders with the choice between allegiance to Paris or to Washington, forcing Bonn on many occasions into uncomfortable splits. But every time a French president unwisely confronted Bonn with the direct choice, it plumped for the latter.

There were no such hesitations when Bonn had to choose between pleasing Moscow and securing the continuing friendship of Washington. Indeed, all successive governments in Bonn have been unconditionally loyal to Washington and the Atlantic alliance. Aware of the burden of Germany's past and the enduring suspicions that even the FRG's closest neighbours and partners continue to harbour, aware also of their own impotence *vis-à-vis* the Warsaw Pact, West German governments consistently treasured their defence and political relationship with Washington above that with any other power, making it the prime pillar of German security policy. They understood that the FRG needed US protection more than any other country in Europe, and that only US generosity and firm leadership prevented Germany's ever-suspicious European partners from putting historical memory before present-day experience.

Despite ups and downs in German intellectuals' attitudes towards the United States, the population of the FRG has generally been consistently pro-American and is likely to remain so. These factors will probably remain with us at least until there is a change of government.

Other European members of NATO

Other European powers also have their particular bilateral relationships with the United States. The non-communist leaders of Italy, for example, have since the mid-1940s sought to draw advantage from aligning themselves with the United States. Italy has sought its own 'special relationship' with America, trying to oust France as chief Mediterranean power of the Atlantic alliance. As France was withdrawing its Mediterranean fleet from NATO command, this was largely possible for Italy, whose policies have, however, more often been characterized by passivity than by leadership ambitions. This is reflected in Italy's contribution to NATO in terms of military spending per GNP, which has been lower than that of comparable countries for many decades. But Italy now feels itself to be in NATO's new front line *vis-à-vis* North Africa, and is keen to bring this critical area to the attention of its allies.

Spain shares this concern. Both states are now doing their utmost to involve other powers in the securing of Mediterranean stability through multilateral negotiations. But whereas Italy favours US involvement, it has rarely played a particularly active role in international security relations since the Second World War. Spain has a specific problem with the United States, which liberal Spaniards see as having been too tolerant of Franco. Spain has therefore negotiated a special arrangement within NATO, which leaves Spanish forces outside the integrated military structure, but involved in all planning committees. To a lesser extent than France, and for a shorter period, Spain has thus also earned fame for its ambiguous support for NATO. The doubts in the US and Britain on the wisdom of choosing Javier Solana, a leading Spanish politician, as new secretary-general of NATO reflected this experience with Spain.[61] Only in July 1994 did Spain complete the infrastructure programmes it committed itself to when it joined the Atlantic Alliance in 1982.[62]

Greece also has a record of irritating, rather than reassuring, its alliance members. Locked in a thousand years of adversity with the Turks, Greece has since the mid-1950s shown more anxiety about its eastern NATO ally than about the Warsaw Pact. Greece is therefore seen as only a lukewarm friend by the United States. Athens is constantly critical of Washington for not coming down harder on Ankara, particularly after the Turkish invasion of north Cyprus in 1974. The Greeks' reiteration of their grievances has severely tried the patience of their NATO allies, particularly the United States. Moreover, even during the Cold War, Papandreou's socialist PASOK government, in particular, in many ways proved extremely uncooperative towards the United States. This did not endear Greece to the Americans (or other NATO allies) and explains why they are not more sympathetic to the Greek side in the long-standing Graeco-Turkish disputes over the Aegean islands and Cyprus.

Despite the black record of its domestic politics, and against the background of Greek uncooperativeness, Turkey has stood out as a particularly willing and loyal NATO ally for the United States. Eager to pull its weight particularly in terms of manpower, and willing to let the United States use its territory for bases of all sorts, Turkey has through its military policy made itself indispensable to the Americans, both during the Cold War and more recently in the Gulf war. The American 'great idealists' have therefore turned a blind eye to Turkish human rights abuses (for example, with regard to minorities and political prisoners) and blatant violations of international agreements.

The United States has other loyal but uncontroversial partners in Europe. Among them are the Netherlands, large among the small powers, punching above its weight as regards military expenditure and armed forces (particularly naval and air forces). There are the two Scandinavian NATO members, Denmark and Norway, which, largely owing to their fear of Germany, have both chosen not to join any purely European defence structure, and always look to America for leadership.

Crucially, they can all more easily accept American leadership than that of any European neighbour. This is as true of Belgium and Portugal as of the medium powers, Britain, France and Germany. Centuries of mutual oppression, rivalry and ever-repeated invocations of memories of former wars, occupation, brutality and injustice have conditioned the Europeans to feel reservations about one another which many of them find difficult to surmount. This is shown by widespread resistance to further European integration, even where there is awareness of common values. Just as many Belgians do not want the European Union to be dominated by France, many Danes would hate the Germans to exercise leadership, while the Dutch government has despaired of Britain's willingness, never mind ability, to do so.[63] Most governments can score points in the battle for electoral approval when they are shown to have defended 'national interests' against 'encroachments' by the European Commission. Even where truly vital interests are concerned, such as defence and security, Europeans are still happier to bring in the respected powerful outside arbiter, the United States, rather than be left to sort themselves out. In a poll in 1994, 42% of British and German respondents said they regarded the United States as their country's most reliable political ally, while only 6% of the British saw the Germans in this role, and only 5% opted for France; 4% of Germans chose the British, with 27% opting for France.[64] This is a crucial feature of the Atlantic Alliance from its founding to the war in Yugoslavia: the European powers would rather submit to US leadership than that of any other European power where it comes to defence. Even in limited contingencies, Europeans want US involvement, and that means leadership; their policies in Bosnia are the latest example of this. They complain about the Americans being too domineering – but in the end, they tend to fall into line behind the United States. They will not, however, follow one another.[65]

US attitudes towards Europe

We have already noted that most settlers in America had fled from something in Europe: poverty, persecution, other hardships. America for them was the promised land, the place where they expected to fare better. This helps us to understand why Americans are often insulted by the notion that they are merely the offspring of Europe, brought up in a remote part of the world. They harbour a deep belief that they are different, and have an identity in their own right. While periodically US leaders assert that theirs is 'a European power',[66] this has been contested more than once from within the same US leadership.[67]

With increasing prosperity in Europe, immigration from this continent to the United States is decreasing while from other continents it is increasing. This means that ever fewer Americans were themselves born in Europe. For them travelling to Europe means little more than visiting any of the great monuments of human civilization. In ten, twenty years' time, a visit to the Taj Mahal or to Borobudur, to Nara or to Angkor Wat, may be a no less emotional experience for American tourists than one to Versailles or Rome.

Indeed, shared popular culture today results more from US exports of television series and cinema films to Europe than from any European influence on America. 'Dallas' and 'Dynasty' are known throughout the world, the majority of films shown in cinemas throughout the European Union were made in Hollywood, and the O. J. Simpson trial made news in Britain, France and Germany. The flow of culture in the other direction is little more than a trickle, although European playwrights and film-makers insert scenes catering for the American market into their products.

The one area where Europe may continue to have an edge in attracting American visitors is education, and here Britain reaps the benefit of the shared language. Efforts are made periodically to strengthen Britain's appeal by providing prestigious grants aimed specifically at Americans, such as the Rhodes scholarships of which President Clinton was a beneficiary, and most recently the Atlantic Fellowships.[68] But the resources that British universities can offer to their own and to foreign students are poor compared with those in the American Ivy League universities. Only the lower fees (rather than pitifully rare grants) can still weigh in the balance of American students' considerations, if it is not simply the adventure of the European culture shock that attracts them.[69]

Talk of common cultural roots does not always appeal to Americans: the Judaeo-Graeco-Christian heritage is increasingly eroded as a basis for a society which tries to be consciously multi-ethnic and multicultural, where increasing numbers of immigrants come from outside Europe and are neither Christian (let alone Anglo-Saxon or Protestant) nor Jewish (see Table 2.1). According to census results for the period 1971–92, of a total of 4.493 million immigrants to the US, only 801,000 or 17.8% came from Europe: 1.633 million (36.3%) came from Asia; 1.645 million (36.6%) from within North America (including Mexico); 284,000 (6.3%) from South America, and 91,000 (2%) from Africa. Censuses predict that Asian and Hispanophone Latin American immigration will increase significantly over the next few decades, and that this will affect the composition and character of the hitherto Anglo-Saxon-dominated US society. Projecting the present immigration rates into the future, by 2050, 22% of US citizens may be of Hispanic (Latin-American) origin (thereby considerably raising the proportion of US society that is Catholic, or at any rate not Protestant), 9% of Asian stock, and 14% might trace their ancestors to Africa, while 56% would be of European descent. Already today, 17.3 million Americans (or 6.9% of the total population) speak Spanish at home.[70] The WASP affinity with Britain, and British-, German- or indeed Scandinavian-derived cultural traits assumed in the past to be typical of US society, may well become less widely shared.

Table 2.1: US population claiming sole or primary European ancestry or ethnic origins

	Million	%
Total population of US	249	100
Total indicating specific foreign ancestry	164.3	66
Total indicating European ancestry (total estimated as having, European ancestry, 1980)	142.6 199.2	57.3 80*
Total British & Irish	54	21.4
German	45.6	18.3
Irish	22.7	9.0
English	22.7	9.0
Italian	11.3	4.5
Polish	6.5	2.6
French	6.2	2.5
Scottish-Irish	4.3	1.7
Dutch	3.5	1.4
Scottish	3.3	1.3
Swedish	2.9	1.2
Norwegian	2.5	1.0
Welsh	1.0	0.4
Other W. European	5.1	2.1
Former Yugoslav	0.8	0.3
3 Baltic states	0.6	0.2
Other East European	3.5	1.4

Source: US Census, 1990.
*US Bureau of the Census, *Statistical Abstract of the United States, 1994* (Washington, DC: 1995), p. 18.

In short, US society, ethnic structure and culture are changing, developing away from their European roots. While there is no reason why this should affect the fundamental values which both Americans and Europeans profess to believe in today, this cultural coming-of-age, or emancipation from European influences, is bound to have some impact on the sentimental side of US–European relations. With reduced European–American migration, ties of kinship and culture will lose some of their previous importance. What will remain is the common values, and common interests with regard to global stability, prosperity and dissemination of democracy and human rights.

Chapter 3

Canada: a transatlantic hinge

> Canadians hold deeply that we must pursue our values internation-
> ally. They want to promote them for their own sake, but they also
> understand that our values and rights will not be safeguarded if they
> are not enshrined throughout the international environment.[1]

Canada's special position in transatlantic relations

The history of Canada and indeed of its relations with Europe is totally
different from that of the US. Canada was not born out of a rejection of
Europe; such a rejection has barely materialized even now. Canada's
identity has to be defined very largely as against that of the United States,
its first direct enemy which in the wars of 1812–14 tried in vain to
conquer its territories. This crucial reserve *vis-à-vis* the US persists, despite
the fact that Canada has much in common with it besides geography:
trade; its multi-ethnic population; the feeling of being a young nation, not
weighed down by history; the European origins of almost all its culture.

Canada's own identity circles elliptically around the two poles of its
historical origins: the heritage of the French colonial status of some parts,
known as *Nouvelle France* (mainly what is today the Province of Quebec,
but also Acadia, later rebaptized Nova Scotia), and that of British
colonial possessions in other less populated areas of North America
(New Brunswick, Prince Edward Island, Newfoundland, British Columbia). Franco-British rivalry for Canada can be traced back as far as the
war of 1756–63, when Britain seized the French colonial towns of
Québec and Montréal, the main settlements of *Nouvelle France*.

A pronounced anti-US spirit came into existence in Canada as early as
1783, when the British–US peace treaty of Versailles induced 40,000

loyalists to leave the United States for Canada. This and other remaining British colonies in North America continued to rely heavily on British protection against expansionist tendencies of its large neighbour to the south. Canada (into which these British colonies were gradually absorbed, from 1867 known as the Dominion of Canada) continued to have particularly close economic relations with Britain. It was only with the Second World War that Canadian exports to the US began to exceed exports to the United Kingdom (see Table 3.1).

The British part of Canada's dual identity has to this day crucially determined its foreign and military policies in particular. Canada was loyal to the United Kingdom during the wars of the twentieth century. In the Boer War, 7,000 Canadian volunteers fought alongside the British; in the First World War, over 600,000 Canadians volunteered to fight with the Entente powers. During the Second World War, Canada dispatched five divisions to Europe, and Canadian forces were permanently stationed in Europe until the end of the Cold War.

It was during the Second World War that the defence triad of Britain, the US and Canada was formed. The particularly close cooperation established at the time between the UK and the United States was thus extended to include Canada, laying the basis for the subsequent shift of the Canadian special defence relationship from London to Washington. After the war, the triad remained in place for intelligence. In some areas of defence it was superseded by the multilateral structures of NATO (in the creation of which Canada played a leading part), while in others it gave way to three exclusive bilateral relationships, among which the US–Canadian and the US–British are arguably the most important. These defence relationships and, above all, NATO as a public forum of defence cooperation, have been and remain crucial for Canada not only in the context of defence but also as channels for influencing the policies of the USA, Britain and other major players in NATO.

Indifference to the British connection in Canada has always been pronounced among the Francophones. While it is spreading further today, it has not given way to an affective preference for rapprochement with the United States, even though trade patterns almost make Canada part of it. Oddly, Quebec is an exception to this, there being a tendency among Quebeckers to be particularly interested in links with the United States.

There is nothing like as close an affinity between Quebec and France as there is between most of the other Canadian provinces (bar, perhaps, the Pacific Province of British Columbia, in many ways isolated from the rest of Canada) and Britain. Hardly any Francophones volunteered during

Table 3.1: Canadian exports and imports (%)
(a) Exports

	1938	1953	1965	1989	1994
USA	32	58.7	56.8	73.2	81.5
UK	40.6	16.2	13.8	2.6	1.5
Germany*	2.2	2	2.2	1.4	1
Japan	2.5	2.9	3.7	6.4	4.3
France				1	0.6

(b) Imports

	1938	1953	1965	1989	1994
USA	62.8	73.5	69.8	65.2	67.7
UK	17.6	10.3	7.4	3.8	2.5
Germany*	1.5	0.8	2.7	2.7	2.2
Japan	0.7	0.3	2.7	7.1	5.6
France				1.5	1.2

Sources: For 1938–65 figures: *Brockhaus Enzyklopädie,* Vol. 9 (Wiesbaden: F.A. Brockhaus, 1970), p. 690; for 1989–94 figures: Canadian government.
*Figures for 1953–89 are for West Germany only.

the two world wars to fight in Europe. The convergence of the interests of the Quebec movement for independence and of the mischievous de Gaulle in 1967 was but short-lived. When the Canadian Prime Minister Pierre Elliott Trudeau tried to woo France (and other European countries) into supporting Canada's closer association with the European Community in the late 1970s and early 1980s, Paris showed little interest. In political terms, just as in matters of trade and investment, France has done little in the last three decades to keep alive any special relationship with Quebec. Yet without the connection with *francophonie*, Quebec would have a narrower literary base to draw on. Its very pronounced French heritage in matters ranging from its political philosophy (the apotheosis of sovereignty, its belief in cultural and civic, not ethnic, nationhood) to its literature gives Quebec a strong, deep-rooted non-Anglo-Saxon identity: all other non-Anglo-Saxon cultures (the Scandinavian, German, Italian, etc.) have been assimilated into the body of the Anglo-Saxon majority culture.

Canada is thus strangely poised between the two continents, like the United States a child of Europe, but unlike it one that has never rejected its parents and has only half-heartedly left home. Canadians see them-selves almost as Europeans, and their greatest disappointment seems to be that Europeans do not give them as much attention as they give to one another or to Canada's big North American neighbour. Trudeau's 'Third Option' plan of associating Canada more closely with the European Community to counterbalance US influence would still, it seems, be the preferred option for the Canadian foreign policy elite, had they not become convinced of the lack of European interest in such an association. Canadian diplomats and statesmen seem to feel and think more European than the Americans, yet they are more inescapably tied to the Americans through both geography and trade (see Table 3.1). They occasionally play the role of a bridge between the United States and Europe, as when their Foreign Secretary Lester Pearson worked so hard on the creation of the Atlantic Alliance, and as Minister of International Trade Roy MacLaren was doing in 1993–5 in his quest for a transatlantic free trade area. But that role of *pontifex transatlanticus* is more often claimed by Britain.

Another role that Canada has consistently chosen to play since the Second World War is that of honest broker in the UN and other inter-national fora. In a whole range of international organizations, Canada has been able to assume the role of the champion of international law and stability.[2] It has been particularly active in arms control. In 1995, work by Canada together with two other Commonwealth countries (Sri Lanka and South Africa) achieved the ice-breaking compromise which made possible the indefinite extension of the Nuclear Non-Proliferation Treaty (NPT).

These activities are based on Canada's values, which are explicitly formulated and extolled, much more than is the case in the United Kingdom. The special joint committee of the Canadian Senate and the House of Commons reviewing Canadian foreign policy formulated these values as follows:

> the practice of dialogue, tolerance and compromise; the commit-ment to an open, democratic society, to human rights and to social and economic justice; responsibility for solving global environmen-tal problems; working for international peace; and helping to ease poverty and hunger in the developing world.[3]

Or, as a Canadian government publication puts it:

> Universal respect for human rights is in Canada's interest. ...
> Democracy promotes stability and prosperity. ... The international

system must be ruled by law not power. ... Sustainable development ... [is] a central component of the Canadian value system.[4]

The attitudes of other countries show that Canada is the United States' best-liked ally, coming before the United Kingdom and a long way before other European or indeed Latin American countries.[5] Britons feel warmly towards Canadians, and Canada is still thought of as an extension of Britain itself, the place of refuge in a catastrophe, a country with which British leaders are happy to share most secret intelligence data and analysis. On the diplomatic stage, Britons know the Canadians to be good team players, imaginative and inventive in the search for compromises that might defuse critical international problems, prepared to commit time and personnel to help solve third parties' problems. Other Europeans in general are kindly disposed towards Canada, but it does tend to slip out of their limited zone of vision, which is mainly directed either inwards or towards the areas of instability to the east and south of the EU. When Europeans look across the Atlantic, the giant United States tends to fill the picture, squeezing its neighbours out. From the perspective of Spain and Portugal, Central and South America form part of the picture, making Canada almost disappear.

This is precisely the Canadians' grievance: they are easily ignored or forgotten by the Europeans. Nevertheless, in their concern not to be left alone with the United States, Canadians continue to show more interest in contacts with Europe than mere trade statistics or security concerns might warrant.

The agony of union

Today, Canada is facing perhaps the gravest internal crisis since the early French colonies fell under British rule. What is at issue is the future of the largely Francophone Province of Quebec, the most self-conscious remainder of the *Nouvelle France*.

A brief glance at the linguistic composition of the Canadian population (see Table 3.2) suggests that it is not too different from that of the US; yet the resulting mix is very particular, its specificity lying in the high percentage of French speakers, concentrated in the former French colonies within Canada.

Chief among these is Quebec, a province separating the mainly English-speaking eastern and western provinces of Canada. In 1774 and on several subsequent occasions during Canada's history, the former French colonies asserted their autonomy *vis-à-vis* their British overlords and

Table 3.2: Linguistic and ethnic composition of Canadian population

Total population (1981):	24, 343, 181		%
Natives:			
Inuit (Eskimos)	23,000	(1980)	
Indians	309,590	(1982)	
English mother tongue	14,918,445		61.3
French " "	6,249,095		25.7
Italian " "	528,775		2.2
German " "	522,855		2.1
Ukrainian " "	292,265		1.2
Chinese " "	224,030		0.9
Eskimo/Indian " "	166,575		0.7
Portuguese " "	165,510		0.8
others " "	1,275,630		5.2

Source: *Der Große Ploetz* (Freiburg: Verlag Ploetz, 1991), p. 1288.

Anglophone neighbours. After a number of constitutional struggles between Quebeckers and the Ottawa government and indeed a series of insurrections with pronounced French-Canadian participation throughout the nineteenth century, the first half of the twentieth century experienced relative calm.

Conflict came to the fore again in the early 1960s, in the wake of economic recession. A Quebecker separatist party under René Lévesque from 1962 demanded greater autonomy for the province, and in 1963 the militant Front de Libération du Quebec (FLQ) was founded. Two years later a leading Quebecker politician, Paul Gérin-Lajoie, publicized his 'Quebec doctrine on international relations', in which he stipulated that every province of Canada had the right to intervene in international affairs where that province was affected, and that this included a say in treaty-making. At the same time, Gérin-Lajoie insisted that Quebec was not simply another province like British Columbia or Nova Scotia, but that Quebeckers constituted a nation in their own right.

In 1967 President de Gaulle poured petrol onto the glowing tinder by calling out to a crowd in the centre of Montreal, 'Vive le Québec libre!' France was prepared to grant the province of Quebec alone a place in *francophonie*, something the Canadian federal government found most difficult to accept. Although Ottawa was prepared to grant wide-ranging concessions, declaring the entire country bilingual (accompanied by measures such as printing all official documents in both languages), and allowing Quebec the right to have independent trade delegations in foreign countries, the separatists were not satisfied. As a minimum, the Quebecker separatists wanted only one language, French, to be spoken in their province.

In autumn 1970, strikes among students and mass demonstrations culminated in bombings and the kidnapping of a British commercial attaché and the Quebecker Minister of Labour by the FLQ; the latter was assassinated, and a state of emergency was proclaimed in Quebec. An uneasy calm was restored. In 1976, René Lévesque and his Parti Québécois (or Péquistes) were brought to power in Quebec. The national government under the French-Canadian Pierre Trudeau managed to delay his call for a referendum, and when it finally took place in May 1980, 59.5% of Quebeckers voted 'no'.[6]

This was followed by a lull lasting for about a decade. Meanwhile the government of Quebec took full advantage of its trade and tourism delegations abroad to build up its own para-diplomatic network not only in Washington, Atlanta, Chicago, Boston, Los Angeles and Mexico City, but also in Brussels, London and Düsseldorf.[7] In July 1990, the Bloc Québécois under Lucien Bouchard was formed, becoming the official opposition in the Canadian federal government after the election of October 1993.

Pressure built up again until a second referendum was held in October 1995 under the leadership of Jacques Parizeau as Prime Minister of Quebec and Lucien Bouchard as opposition leader in Ottawa. This time, the result was even closer: only 50.6% voted against the proposal, with 49.4% voting for it, the difference amounting to 50,000 votes.[8] As a result of their narrow defeat, the separatists now seem unwilling to abandon their cause. Bouchard has succeeded Parizeau as Prime Minister of Quebec, and is expected to prepare another referendum in the foreseeable future.[9]

The struggle between Quebecker separatists and the rest of the country strikes one as all too European, even though Quebeckers like to deny that the same forces of ethnic nationalism are at work in their province as in Europe, where the cancerous quest for separatist self-determination has progressively divided multi-ethnic states since the invention of ethnic (as opposed to civic, democratic) nationalism early in the nineteenth century. While the latest wave of Quebecker separatism has not (so far) led to bloodshed and is predominantly democratic in tone, there are disquieting little signs of ethnic intolerance within Quebec of the so-called 'allophones', those whose first language is neither French nor English. And it is important to note that in Canada, too, non-European immigra-

Table 3.3: Immigration to Canada 1994 by countries of origin

Total new citizens	219,450
United Kingdom, British Dependent Territories, British Overseas Citizens	38,696
Former Warsaw Pact	12,293
Other west, north and south European (including neutrals)	8,557
of whom French	2,735
Former Yugoslavia	6,807
United States	5,741
Latin America	11,160
Caribbean	9,683
Africa (excluding Arab countries)	8,994
Arab world	10,980
India, Pakistan, Bangladesh, Sri Lanka	30,815
Other Asian (excl. Russia, Israel, Arab and Turkic countries)	50,696
of whom, Chinese	20,449
Filipino	19,100
Vietnamese	5,021
Other (incl. stateless)	7,239

Source: Canadian 1994 census figures, made available by the Canadian High Commission in London.

tion is rising faster than European; only a very small percentage of new immigrants (around 4%) is Francophone (see Table 3.3).

It must also be remembered that Canada has a complex relationship with its large Anglophone neighbour to the south, fearing cultural absorption (quite apart from economic absorption through the North American Free Trade Association, NAFTA).[10] Their bilingual culture is part of the difference which gives Canadians the assurance that they can protect themselves against such assimilation. It is not least for this reason that Anglophone Canadians are surprisingly tolerant of the Quebec separatists, and surprisingly reluctant to divorce from a part of Canada that has a considerable budget deficit and economic problems.

The overall effect of this crisis (and of the concept of a common Canadian national identity) effectively means that the federal government of Canada has to some extent been paralysed by its concerns about the future of the federation. Quebec is among the three largest policy issues for Canada, alongside the United States and the creation of jobs;

there are some who see Quebec as the greatest of these problems.[11] Until the beginning of 1996, Prime Minister Jean Chrétien's largely francophone cabinet, with the exception of the Minister of International Trade, Roy MacLaren, seemed forced to concentrate more on domestic than on foreign affairs. The situation is more hopeful since the government reshuffle of January 1996.[12]

Domestic issues now dominate Canada's politics. Quebec's crisis of identity will probably loom large in the coming few years and another referendum is expected. High-profile foreign policies that require domestic consensus and could lead to major domestic debates are unlikely to be adopted in this climate. For example, there is considerable pressure against any increase in aid and for a concentration on fewer recipient countries.[13]

Yet Canada's able representatives will undoubtedly continue to act as honest brokers and active team players in international fora such as the UN, as they have done in the past with considerable success. The NAFTA negotiations (concluded in 1994), work for the indefinite extension of the NPT, and most recently the MacLaren initiatives show that notwithstanding its internal crisis, Canada is capable of pursuing and indeed playing a leading role in the negotiation of ambitious multilateral schemes, as long as these are not very controversial at home. Indeed, the consensus among Canada's elected representatives is that their country should continue to play a considerable role, alongside 'like-minded' powers, in furthering peace and security in international affairs.[14]

Wall to the demise of the Soviet Union. What was this new world that was rising from the ashes of the Cold War before our very eyes? Were all the fears of war that had hung over Europe and America since the 1940s vanishing like a bad dream? Had a new age of peace started? Could defence expenditures be cut and conscription ended? Had defensive alliances like NATO outlived their function?

Those who saw NATO merely as an anti-Soviet defence alliance asserted that it had.[3] To some, it was the triumph of the nations, which de Gaulle had predicted would finally overcome all alliances and ideologies. Others proclaimed that the hour of a European defence strategy independent from the United States had come.

Again others, aware of NATO's base of common values, and of the North Atlantic Treaty's non-military clauses, advocated its wider interpretation. The potential of Article 2 (political and economic cooperation, the dissemination of democracy) and Article 4 (consultation on security issues other than direct aggression against a member) was recognized.[4]

Still others turned to universalism, putting their hopes in a new UN, which over forty years after its creation had begun to play the role envisaged by its founding fathers. All were forcefully reminded of the continued existence of war by Saddam Hussein, but the Gulf war seemed to culminate in the triumph of what the United Nations could do. All shared the hope that the end of the Cold War meant that the rules of interstate behaviour (in which violence is not a legitimate tool to settle disputes) which had operated among the North Atlantic countries for the previous four decades would now spread to eastern Europe, and perhaps even beyond.

With the thawing of Cold War ice some of the beliefs with which whole generations had grown up seemed likely to melt away. Which of the lodestars of the Cold War were still to be followed? Which of the beacons, which themselves seemed to be floating on drift ice, rather than being anchored on firm land? The rationale for beliefs had to be re-examined, and the results produced by different individuals and in different governments went off in many different directions. All agreed that economic aid for the East was crucial, but all had their own economic problems as a worldwide recession set in. Some were looking for a new role for NATO while others sought means to integrate Eastern Europe into Western security. For some, the prerequisite for this was the dissolution of NATO; for others, NATO's continued existence was a vital precondition; others again did not think security was a problem any longer. Some wanted to extend the European Union to prevent it from being 'deepened' institutionally; others wanted it to 'deepen' precisely because they wanted to extend it, but feared for its effectiveness if it was extended without deepening.

The optimism that had seized Europe took a decisive downward turn in 1991, when after the triumph of the West in the Gulf war, Yugoslavia experienced a resurgence of the nationalism that had bloodied Europe so horribly in the late nineteenth and first half of the twentieth centuries. The fear spread that this would not be the only instance of Europe's return to its own bloody past. Clearly, the age of peace had not yet arrived.[5]

Again, reactions differed as to how these new security problems were to be tackled. The Gulf war had left the French, in particular, bitter over the experience of their own impotence, and the irrelevance of European institutions. For a variety of reasons, other European countries, too, welcomed the idea that it was up to the Europeans to deal with this problem. There were certainly those in the US leadership who were content to leave this emergency to Europe to sort out. But it failed to do so – whoever or whatever is to blame. The result was that the boundless optimism of 1990 gave way not only to post-achievement depression, but also to tensions within NATO, scepticism about the further integration of Europe, general malaise.

Russia

If anything is symptomatic of this malaise, it is the perception of developments since December 1991 in the Commonwealth of Independent States, and most particularly in Russia. One could naïvely assume that with the Cold War over, all liberal democracies throughout the world must now share all major security concerns, and must therefore be inclined to join together in working for peace and stability. For any believer in the virtues of democracy, all should be well as long as Russia's elections are free.[6] At this juncture one may hope that Russia will continue, albeit stumbling and halting, on the road towards stabilizing its infant democracy, turning into an *état de loi*, establishing a viable free-market economy, and feeding and housing its huge population without doing further irreparable damage to a ruthlessly exploited environment. It is clearly in the best interests of Europeans, North Americans and indeed all other neighbours of Russia that its huge social and economic problems should be solved without its political culture degenerating into greater authoritarianism, nationalism and expansionism. But whatever might or might not be in the interest of external powers, there is little if anything they can do that would have *decisive* positive influence on Russia, given its size in terms of geography and population, and the related size of its problems. There are, however, negative effects which should be avoided. However much one might dislike the fact, neither Russia nor indeed China can be ignored or pushed around. The sheer size of Russia's military forces and nuclear arsenals makes it most dangerous.

Yet the values of the North Atlantic nations were severely tried by their own failure to intervene against the human rights abuses in Eastern Europe during the Cold War.[7] These values could not be reconciled with granting recognition to a new Russian sphere of influence (or, worse, unhindered military intervention) in the 'near abroad', were it not for the lasting Cold War truth that one's best values cannot be defended in open war against a nuclear power. The Cold War realization thus holds that whatever horrors occur within Russia, the things the North Atlantic nations can do to intervene are limited at best. Also, the open sores of the body of the former Soviet Union testify that the wounds left by the dismembering of the USSR have become infected with crime and nationalism. Not only Moscow is to blame for the bloodshed in Nagorno Karabakh, or even the origins of the war with Chechenia.

Whatever the regime in Russia, it is in the collective interests of the North Atlantic nations that it be prevailed upon to cooperate, through recognizing shared interests with them, on as many issues as possible. It should be possible to convey the message that it is a matter of common interest (and would not cause Russia to 'lose out') for central and eastern Europe to become more prosperous and for its systems of government to remain or become politically stable.

The integration of a number of states in that area into the European Union should theoretically not be a problem from the Russian point of view.[8] In these countries, armed forces visibly reconfigured and trained for territorial defence on the one hand, and low-intensity operations in multinational peacekeeping operations on the other, should also appear non-controversial, even if they receive substantial aid in training and equipment from the North Atlantic nations.

Against this background Russia's admission to the Council of Europe deserves applause, notwithstanding the understandable reservations following Russian actions in Chechenia. It is also thoroughly understandable and probably sensible that the Council of Europe's parliamentary assembly voted to give the United States observer status.[9] As long as Russia is not a well-established, mature democracy, any role it plays in Europe continues to need an American counterweight. But expecting it to accept NATO expansion is asking a great deal of any democratic government in

Moscow, which unavoidably looks weak compared with its Soviet pre-decessors. Russian culture characteristically has little respect for any-body claiming authority without an aura of inflexible might. Ability and readiness to compromise are admired in few parts of the world.

Russia also has another, indirect effect on European–American rela-tions: all US–Russian bilateralism since the 1950s has been seen as dangerous by the Europeans, who worried about being sacrificed in some superpower deal.[10] In the future, as in the past, US–Russian bilateralism will put strains on transatlantic relations. Yet paradoxically, just as they did during the Cold War, Europeans worry even more when relations between the two giants are frosty.[11]

Weapons of mass destruction and missile proliferation, international terrorism and crime

Whatever the political hue of future governments of Russia, one might draw comfort from the fact that if they are in the least rational, and if ideology does not again lead them to have other priorities, they will recognize the need for cooperation with the North Atlantic nations at least so as to give Russia's economy an optimal chance to pick up through injections of technology and perhaps even limited foreign investment; and from the fact that certain interests – in the prevention of nuclear proliferation, of the spread of other weapons of mass destruction (WMD) and of missiles – were shared even by the mortal enemies on both sides of the Iron Curtain during the Cold War itself.

Certainly, despite the Chemical Weapons Convention of 1993 and the indefinite extension in 1995 of the NPT, the danger of proliferation in these areas has not gone away. Nor has the threat of the proliferation of crucial dual-use technologies, of the development and use of biological weapons or of the use of missiles to transport WMD.[12] Indeed, missiles with mere conventional charges can cause considerable anxiety, as shown by the experience with the German V1 and V2 rockets in the Second World War and Iraqi missiles in the 1990–91 Gulf war. The development of missile and WMD technology, whether legally or illegally procured, whether forbidden or sanctioned by the NPT of 1968, continues to pose the most direct military threat to both North America and the EU coun-tries. It is thus clearly in the interest of both that they should cooperate in all possible ways to contain this danger.[13]

Here, as in many other fields, we see a pattern emerging in which only certain countries show an active military commitment to cooperation, even if all NATO and EU members show determination to cooperate on non-military aspects. The countries able and potentially willing to implement NATO's policy of preventing proliferation[14] on a military level are the three Atlantic members of the United Nations Security Council (UNSC). These are also the three countries with nuclear weapons and a national force projection capacity (although Britain and France have very limited capacity compared with the United States). Though all five permanent members of the UNSC – all nuclear weapons states – are committed to the upholding of the NPT, and though even China showed some willingness to cooperate in the 1991–4 crisis over potential North Korean nuclear development, it is not certain that they would be willing to cooperate on all proliferation issues.

Russia is most likely to seek cooperation in this area with the three Atlantic powers, the US, Britain and France. The USSR was among the first countries to press for nuclear development constraints, from its backing of the Baruch Plan of 1947 to support for non-proliferation and test moratoria. Russia, like the Soviet Union before it, supports the idea of complete nuclear disarmament, a proposal which consistently foundered on NATO's perception of its own weakness in the face of Warsaw Pact conventional forces and on its belief in nuclear deterrence. In view of the absence in Europe, the Middle East or South Asia of any massive land forces poised to attack the territory of the former Soviet Union, Russia has indeed most to fear from long-range missile attacks with WMD warheads. It is therefore likely to continue the USSR's policy of consistent opposition (since the late 1950s) to any nuclear proliferation. The three Atlantic permanent members should in theory be able to find common ground for cooperation with Moscow in this area, although the prospects are looking worse now than two years ago. In view of Russian national pride, it will be important that Moscow is not seen merely to be following the Atlantic powers' lead (as during the Gulf war and over the North Korean breach of NPT commitments). In the domestic Russian debate this is increasingly regarded as an unacceptable surrender of leadership.

China is the more unpredictable variable in this context. In the past, it has contributed significantly to the development of missile programmes in both Latin America and the Middle East. Even now, China seems to be inspiring its neighbours with new bouts of fear as to its future intentions; this is not only leading to military build-ups in Southeast Asia but is also worrying India. China is said to want to join a complete test ban agreement at the end of 1996, but significant forces in the Chinese government oppose any such commitment.

In this area, then, cooperation should not be confined to actions by NATO members. Indeed, in seeking Moscow's vital cooperation, it would probably be highly unwise to try to tackle the issue of proliferation in a way that excludes Russia. It would also be worthwhile for Russia, the United States, Britain, France and their allies to expend considerable energy on trying to convince the Chinese that cooperation in this area would be in their own interests. But on non-military levels, in order to prevent the smuggling of fissile material or technology, extensive cooperation between the governments of practically all countries opposing nuclear proliferation would be required, as just about any country could be used for the illicit transit of such materials. A significantly expanded and deepened cooperation through the EU's third pillar (which includes cooperation between police forces) would be beneficial here, but it would also help if this were extended beyond the EU to other trustworthy countries, particularly the United States and Canada.

On a lower level of integration, it would be extremely valuable to achieve more cooperation in monitoring international terrorist movements and dangerous materials in other member states of the Organization for Security and Cooperation in Europe (OSCE). As this comprises the former Warsaw Pact members and the states of the former Soviet Union, as well as NATO members and former neutrals, this would take preventive measures to one potentially crucial source of trouble.

In all the central and east European countries, there has been a staggering increase in crime, and their governments are struggling to master this novel situation. The effectiveness of their efforts is severely checked by the international connections of criminal groups; this points to the need for transborder cooperation. While efforts in this area could be a welcome spin-off from cooperation on export controls, the danger posed by terrorist groups, in many respects indistinguishable from criminal networks, should not be forgotten. We do not need to imagine airport-literature scenarios about terrorist use of WMD to see the importance of countering this threat: the mere conventional explosives used by terrorists in the attack on a government office in Oklahoma City, the bombings in Paris and Atlanta, and the chemical poison attack on the Tokyo underground system, all during 1995–6, sufficed to inspire fear and despondency in these highly developed – and thus highly vulnerable – societies. The same considerations apply to the fight against international drug dealers. Here, too, international cooperation would be extremely helpful, and again this need not, indeed should not, be confined to NATO members.

Theatre missile defence?
If the danger of further proliferation of WMD and longer-range missiles cannot be excluded, then the question of a numerically limited anti-ballistic missile (ABM) defence system continues to impose itself. During the Cold War, the issue was discussed twice at length, first in the 1960s and again in the 1980s. On the first occasion, the consensus emerged among both the superpowers that fully-fledged ABM systems would not be desirable, as enemies would have the incentive to try to swamp them by firing ever more missiles. This would have encouraged a further missile build-up, which both superpowers began to regard as pernicious. Moreover, an ABM system might have gone a long way towards neutralizing the arsenals of the smaller nuclear powers.

The same considerations led Britain and France to fear that a new technological race in space might be sparked off by the American Strategic Defense Initiative (SDI) in the 1980s. The economic inability of the Soviet Union to sustain this lap in the arms race is thought to have contributed to President Gorbachev's decision to bring back detente; the reduction of the perceived outside pressure on the Warsaw Pact was crucial in allowing the centrifugal forces within it to become predominant, leading to its collapse and that of the Soviet Union. In consequence, the perceived need for the SDI waned. But the general idea of some missile defence, albeit scaled down several times in the late 1980s to less ambitious and costly systems, survived, to be rekindled by the Gulf war experience.[15] By February 1995 Secretary of State Warren Christopher and Defense Secretary William Perry could note that the US was 'building effective theater defense systems ... We are conducting a broad research and development program that will, in a few years, be able to deploy a national missile defense system whenever a threat emerges.'[16] That the Russians are significantly less keen on such a scheme is a source of US–Russian tensions; indeed it was put forward by Moscow as a reason why the Strategic Arms Reduction Treaty, START II, might not be ratified.[17]

The rationale for ABMs has shifted decisively since the end of the Cold War. No longer would such a programme be directed against an opponent which could easily overburden a defence system with its vast arsenal. With a putative success rate of 90%, as was often argued by US strategists in the 1960s and the 1980s, even the few enemy missiles reaching their targets could destroy several cities, an unbearable loss.

But now an ABM system might be directed at adversaries with only a very limited number of missiles. These would presumably be of first-generation (that is, very imprecise) technology, requiring large, immobile value targets, such as cities. With fewer than ten missiles fired by such an aggressor, a 90% chance of intercepting them could mean the difference between total defence and total catastrophe.

An ABM system protecting against such a threat would be useful to all who might find themselves threatened – not excluding Russia, or indeed Japan, South Korea, Taiwan, etc. If installed, however, it would substantively alter the significance of the arsenals of France, Britain and China. The acquisition of an ABM system by Russia would challenge the British and French belief in deterrence of a superpower by a small nuclear power, and if both superpowers acquired ABM systems, China would have to depart from its *de facto* policy of nuclear sufficiency if it wanted to continue to hold Russia and the United States in check with its nuclear arsenal. The roles of British and French nuclear weapons, even jointly, would need redefinition: they would barely as much as *contribute* to NATO defence.[18]

The question of whether, in the changed strategic circumstances, it would be worthwhile for Britain to replace its new (and last remaining) nuclear system, the submarine-based Trident missiles, when the issue arises, would probably be influenced quite decisively by this considera-tion. If Britain decided not to replace Trident, it would find itself as dependent on the United States as its other NATO allies, except for France, have been so far.

For France, where nuclear matters have become the core of its beliefs about itself, its sovereignty, independence and role in the world, abandon-ing nuclear power status would be even more acrimonious. But there would be little that France alone could do to offset a Russian ABM shield.[19]

It is only in dealing with a new proliferator, that is a substantially inferior nuclear power, that British and French nuclear forces could provide additional security (through the deterrent threat of nuclear repris-als) to their own populations and perhaps to EU partners. Both countries have hitherto strenuously avoided casting nuclear weapons in this new role, emphasizing their conviction that deterrence only works among adversaries who have shared the learning experience of the first decades of the Cold War.[20]

Both countries are also determined not to allow any doubts to arise as to whether a non-Russian nuclear (or other WMD) threat against parts of NATO Europe would trigger US involvement. Although the North Atlantic Treaty was concluded against one shared, large political and military threat only (the USSR, which became a nuclear power within six months of the signing of the NAT), its text is general enough to pledge US and Canadian support to the Treaty's European signatories wherever a threat might come from (and even if it does not affect North America directly). Americans are less likely to hesitate to stand by their European allies if these are threatened by a country that cannot reach North America with its missiles, than they are if it could wipe out New York as easily as Lampedusa.

The best of the worst-case scenarios of facing a nuclear proliferator would of course be for the nuclear powers to deal with it without recourse to their own nuclear weapons.[21] Cooperation among the UNSC Permanent Five (P5) is more easily imaginable in such non-nuclear counter-proliferation measures, and is even plausible where Britain, France and the United States are concerned. But infinitely more likely is cooperation between the three Atlantic powers only. This provokes more general reflection on security policy in interstate relations.

The return of the great powers

The immediate post-Cold War euphoria about the possibilities of a new world order underwritten by the UN has passed. The optimism and the flux of 1989–92, and the weakness of the USSR/Russia (and indeed China), could have been used to transform the UN into a system capable of reaching binding decisions even if the Security Council were blocked through the veto of one of its permanent members. The United States, Britain and France, as the other permanent members of the UNSC, might have liked to see Russia and China bound in this way, but they were far from prepared to make the corresponding sacrifice of part of their own freedom. Thus the option of a new international order was never seriously discussed. While the Gulf war showed the UN Security Council at its best, reaching consensus on authorizing the military operations that led to the liberation of Kuwait and the defeat of Iraq, the Yugoslav war illustrated that the most fundamental flaw of the oligarchic rule of the P5 had not been a mere Cold War phenomenon.

Sadly, the UNSC showed itself unwilling to take on a peace-making mission in a context where no recognized national borders had been violated and where no clearly definable national unities were in conflict.[22] Moreover, the UNSC became the forum not only of the three Atlantic powers' disagreements with Russia (China showing some minimal cooperativeness) but also of disagreement between the United States on the one hand, and Britain and France on the other, on how to handle the Yugoslav war. Risk assessments, willingness to become involved with ground forces, and views on what might be done to end the fighting differed sharply, while different degrees of commitment to the resolution of the crisis pointed to possible future divergences. This disagreement in turn has deeply affected the Atlantic Alliance, as we shall see presently.

Moreover, the fact that the UN's authorities took seriously their mandate (received from the UNSC) to monitor and intervene in the conflict was represented as counterproductive. When the principal theatre of the Yugoslav war shifted from Slovenia and Croatia to Bosnia, controversy surrounded the role of the UN High Commissioner for Refugees, Yasushi Akashi, particularly, and what was seen as his interference in the application of the UNSC's policies by the military of the states that had agreed to execute UN policy. This conflict of interests and the clash of competences shows some similarity with the disagreements between the European Commission and the national governments of EU member states. In both cases, the governments of the member states (or at least of the UNSC members) collectively agreed at one point to set up institutions acting in the interest of the collectivity (the European Commission and the UN's administration and commissioners). In both cases, governments of the member states later expressed dismay that these institutions and their representatives then tried to carry out the task with which they had been charged.[23]

In the UN (as in the EU) the hopes of integrationists were dashed: the UN will continue to function as the lowest common denominator of the interests of the nation-states that are permanent members of the UNSC, and the focus of policy-making has returned squarely to national governments. From the high hopes of creating a UN standing army, expressed by UN Secretary-General Boutros Boutros-Ghali in mid-1992 in his *Agenda for Peace*,[24] we have returned to concert-of-power politics, nineteenth-century style. The members of the concert are the three Atlantic allies, the USA, Britain and France, plus Russia and China as their reluctant partners. Where we have identified an ever-growing need for international cooperation to fight problems and dangers common to more and more countries, the present predominating tendency in international relations is a return to nineteenth-century European patterns of state rivalry and *ad hoc* coalitions, based on limited coincidences of selfish national designs. Even the US seems to be succumbing to this temptation, perhaps for the first time since Theodore Roosevelt.

This tendency has crucial consequences for the future of transatlantic relations. It initiated or at least reflected a new phase in the paradoxical coexistence of two mutually exclusive concepts: the universalist-legitimist and the Hobbesian. The former continues to drive the quest for legitimacy of action (particularly military action) taken by the great-power concert. Legitimacy can be established only if action is sanctioned by the UN (or OSCE, which derives its legitimacy from the UN Charter) and conforms with its Charter. This enshrines the one universally accepted set of principles that exists to guide international relations, in that every member of the UN signs up to it when joining.

The latter, the Hobbesian concept, recognizes nothing but force, and the schools of thinking derived from it see any form of cooperation merely as *ad hoc* agreements by purely selfish forces on issues on which their selfish interests happen to coincide. The more optimistic among them tend to argue that there has been so much coincidence of interest even among the bitter enemies, the USSR and the United States, that the areas of convergence of interests among the great powers today provide a sufficiently large basis on which to build relative stability in the international system.

What we find in practice, not only within the UN and its dependent regimes (such as arms control regimes or the OSCE), but also among the North Atlantic nations, is an awkward compromise between the two concepts. While on the one hand business is clearly conducted between the great powers only, on the other hand a gloss of legitimacy is always sought for resulting action, by appealing to the UN, the OSCE, or to NATO to bless it with a policy statement. Every time, this leads to lobbying and arm-twisting behind the scenes, and to threats that the United States (sometimes with its closest allies) will resort to unilateralism. But notwithstanding its many unilateral operations, the US has since 1945 preferred a multilateral approach, and continues to do so: the threat of going it alone is usually the big stick that is wielded to persuade other powers to support an operation in return for some influence on its conduct.

In the UNSC, this means that policy-making continues to be a process of haggling among the P5, in which appeals to common interests are intermingled with threats of unilateral action or vetoes. Within this five-way process, a position agreed among the Atlantic powers, the US, France and Britain, is of course a valuable asset. In itself it is not, however, a guarantee of success. Nor is it important on this level (at any rate before any reform of the UNSC) what other North Atlantic nations think. The smaller NATO members can now be considered as something between free-riders and petition-list fillers: the larger the number of signatures on a petition list, the greater its aura of popular representativeness.

Smaller nations can still prevent a consensus from emerging within NATO, and they might themselves reduce its clout by abstaining from contributing to joint action – not that their contributions are as crucial as they were when NATO's task was to stop a Warsaw Pact advance *anywhere*. But even during the Cold War, NATO policy- and strategy-making was able to accommodate some degree of disagreement (as 'footnote' cases in which individual powers declared their reservations about the joint position or through the withdrawal of certain powers from a common policy, e.g. France with regard to NATO strategy between 1966 and 1991). This tolerance for disagreement is growing considerably now that NATO is turning into a legitimizing label for the action of the United States in concert with Britain and France, with perhaps a few Canadian, Dutch, Italian, Spanish or even German volunteers here and there.

This ability to accommodate disagreement is lacking in the European Union. The EU's second pillar, comprising the Common Foreign and Security Policy (CFSP), has been severely handicapped by its self-imposed rule of consensus, which is much more stringent than in NATO, as there is no one power within it exercising forceful leadership that is also accepted by all the other powers. And forceful leadership is necessary, as the history of NATO shows, to bring about consensus. Without it, any degree of convergence on policies is likely to be inadequate as a foundation for active policy.

Hobbesians would argue that the minimal success of both the EU's CFSP and the OSCE is due not least to the absence of a Security Council-type oligarchy of great powers which decide on policy and impose it on the smaller members. The creation of a security council for the OSCE has been proposed repeatedly. Proposals aiming at the collective representation of the EU in such a security council have been opposed vigorously by the United Kingdom and France. Attempts were made to harmonize policies between Britain, France and Germany on key issues (CFSP, European defence, monetary union, etc.) prior to the 1996 Intergovernmental Conference (IGC); but these attempts had little success. Proposals that envisage a security council consisting of the EU great powers have understandably evoked little enthusiasm among the smaller powers. And as universalists would observe, neither the proposal for great-power consensus nor one for a *directoire à trois* or more deals with the fact that it is the great powers themselves which differ most profoundly on major policy issues.

In all these organizations, the crucial obstacle to more effective decision-making remains the determination of the United States, Britain, France and Russia to refuse to accept the legitimacy of a decision made against their express wishes. In the OSCE, the requirement of consensus minus one allows for slightly greater flexibility, but so far no decision has ever been arrived at in this forum against the wishes of the four great powers mentioned. This does not mean that the four have scruples about imposing their own policies on smaller powers, or indeed that they have problems with an unequal system which gives them the veto, but not the lesser powers (in the style of the UNSC). But all four are determined to reserve for themselves the option of unilateral action, while refusing to allow others to act without their blessing. These double standards remain a crucial feature of great-power behaviour in international relations. They have important implications for the future of the Atlantic Alliance itself.

Germany: the reluctant rise of a great power

The great powers under discussion so far have been particularly the United States, Britain, France and Russia. From the point of view of economic and political weight, Germany must also be mentioned in this category, whether or not it is the express design of the German government to play a great-power role. The Federal Republic is still governed by the political parties (and indeed by the same Chancellor) which were in power before unification. None of the values guiding German foreign policy have changed, just as the elites have not changed. Below this, however, the society itself is undergoing changes which have already affected Germany's role in interstate affairs.

The integration of 16.1 million new citizens, coming from a radically different political culture, into the Federal Republic of Germany (which at the time of unification in 1990 had some 63.6 million citizens) is only beginning to show its full impact. The East German infrastructure was found drastically wanting in many respects and badly in need of modernization. The task of modernization proved considerably larger than expected, and the cost had been significantly underestimated. It is sometimes even argued that the cost of German unification not only to the Federal Republic's government but also to countries linked to the FRG through European Union membership contributed to the recession in Europe (even though the negative trend in world economic growth clearly started in 1989).[25]

Prognoses differ as to whether the new *Länder* will quickly become prosperous through the large-scale injection of private and public investment and infrastructural modernization. Though this seems a real possibility, it will take longer for the German state budget to recover from the cost of unification (and paying for the withdrawal of Soviet forces from

East Germany). Nevertheless, despite these costs, the Federal Republic continues to be on balance the greatest net contributor to the EU's budget, with almost five times the sum put in by the next largest.[26] This is beginning to be regarded as unsustainable within the German government. The expenses involved in wanting to put financial sweeteners in the direction of Russia to obtain its agreement on NATO enlargement, wanting to help other EU members reduce their budget deficits to meet the criteria for entering the European Economic and Monetary Union (EMU), and wanting Germany itself to be able to reduce its deficit to meet the EMU criteria cannot continue indefinitely.

On the domestic political front, superficial effects of unification include two new small political parties added to the spectrum of German politics: the remaining members of the alliance of parties which brought about the fall of the GDR (Bündnis 90), and the former Communist Party, rechristened the Party of Democratic Socialism, which is still scoring around 16–23% in local elections in eastern Germany. Yet in general, the majority of East Germans have integrated themselves into the pre-existing political spectrum of the FRG.

There are some noteworthy differences between Eastern and Western concerns in Germany. Both West and East Germans were re-educated by their occupation powers, but more importantly still by their own experience of the double defeat of 1918 and 1945, to reject the earlier German apotheosis of the military and of power. To Germans in both East and West who were forced to reflect on the lessons of the first half of the twentieth century, all war seems evil, with the exception at best of self-defence on their own territory.

But both states were prevailed upon by their allies to build up armies that were integrated into the military systems of their blocs, and were imbued with antipathy towards the enemy (the 'enemy image', as German peace researchers liked to call it). Thus during the Cold War, only a small minority in the FRG (since the 1980s, mainly supporters of the Greens) favoured withdrawal of the FRG from NATO (see Table 4.1). East Germans, however, were raised with the 'enemy image' of NATO as an aggressive pact, and of West Germany as the heir to the fascist empire of Hitler, backed by an imperialist United States. There are still traces of this belief in the attitude of East Germans to the Bundeswehr, NATO and the United States. The resurgence of the pacifist left wing of the Social Democratic opposition party, culminating in the election of Oskar Lafontaine as the party leader, may have been made possible by East German opinion.

Table 4.1: German views of NATO, 1956–94

Opinion polls conducted in West Germany only:
(a) Question: 'All in all, does NATO have more advantages or disadvantages for us West Germans?'

	1956	1959	1971	1979
	%	%	%	%
More advantages	29	43	47	48
Undecided	28	26	29	32
More disadvantages	11	6	9	7
Don't know what NATO is	32	25	15	13
	100	100	100	100

Source: Elisabeth Noelle-Neumann, Institut für Demoskopie, Allensbach (ed.), *The Germans: Public Opinion Polls, 1967–1980* (Westport, CT: Greenwood Press, 1981), p. 435.

(b) Question: 'Do you think that NATO is essential for German security?'

	1981	1983	1988	1990	1991 West	1991 East	1992 West	1992 East	1994 West	1994 East
Agree (%):	62	86	76	53	69	43	64	35	75	60

Sources: USIA, cited in Ronald D. Asmus, *Germany in Transition: National Self-Confidence and International Relations,* RAND Note N-3522-AF (Santa Monica, CA.: RAND, 1992), p. 16; Ronald D. Asmus, *Germany's Geopolitical Maturation: Public Opinion and Security Policy in 1994* (Santa Monica, CA: RAND for the Friedrich Naumann Foundation, 1995), p. 18.

In consequence, views differ even today in West and East Germany on the desirability of complete US troop withdrawal from Germany. It is worth noting in this context that in 1988, prior to reunification and to the possibility that Western forces might remain in Germany while Soviet forces withdrew, an opinion poll conducted in West Germany alone showed that 76% of those asked favoured the withdrawal of all forces from Germany, 9% said they would regret it, and 15% were undecided.[27] Even shortly after reunification, both east and west Germans favoured the total withdrawal of all foreign forces from Germany. Once Soviet forces had withdrawn, however, more than half of all Germans – the highest proportion since the fall of the Wall – responded that they wanted

Table 4.2: German attitudes towards US troop withdrawal

	1990		1991		1993		Nov. 1994	
	West	East	West	East	West	East	West	East
A limited number of US troops should remain (%)	41	13	43	12	47	15	64	24
All US troops should withdraw (%)	46	79	49	84	46	80	29	74

Sources: Asmus, *Germany in Transition*, p. 19; Asmus, *Germany's Geopolitical Maturation*, p. 22.

US troops to stay (see Table 4.2).[28] This seems to indicate that in west Germany, support for a total withdrawal of foreign forces was influenced by the perception of an inevitable linkage of Soviet force withdrawals and Western force withdrawals, and was not purely a function of how easily or badly the population got on with foreign NATO forces in their area. Once the Red Army troops had withdrawn, west German support for continued presence of US forces rose significantly.

Interestingly, the population along the western side of what used to be the inner German border, an area which had known the densest NATO force deployment, was less keen on the withdrawal of foreign (in that area, US and British) forces than the areas further to the west. In the area around Koblenz and Trier (near the French border, in the former French occupation zone, with French forces stationed not far away), the highest polls in favour of the continued presence of foreign forces was found.[29] But with regard to German attitudes towards America, it is worth noting that the sentimental and ideological affinity between the two countries is underpinned by economic incentives: the highest German investment abroad – DM66.7 billion – is in the United States.[30] German business interest in North America thus continues to be solid.

In opinion polls conducted in 1993, 72% of all Germans regarded themselves as pro-American, with only 25% declaring themselves anti-American.[31] (See also Table 4.3.)

Turning back to the pacifism which has been strong in both parts of Germany since 1945 (taking the form of neutralism in the related country of Austria), Germany has since 1990 undergone a profound transformation. There is no apparent increase of militarism or return of any of the old

Table 4.3: German views of the United States

Opinion polls conducted in West Germany only:
Question: 'Generally speaking, do you like the Americans, or don't you like them particularly?'

	1957	1961	1967	1975	1980	1988
	%	%	%	%	%	%
Like them	39	51	47	42	51	41
Undecided	37	33	29	37	27	43
Not particularly	24	16	24	21	22	16
	100	100	100	100	100	100

Sources: Data for 1957–80: Elisabeth Noelle-Neumann, *The Germans: Public Opinion Polls, 1967–1980*, p. 420; 1988: SINUS and Friedrich Ebert Foundation for STERN, *Sowjetische und amerikanische Politik im Urteil der Deutschen in der Bundesrepublik* (Munich: SINUS, 1988), p. 16.

evils associated with the disproportionate respect given to the military in Prussia in the nineteenth century and in Germany between 1871 and 1945. And yet German public and leadership opinion has evolved on the issue of German military action. During the Gulf war it was still seen as entirely unacceptable by German public opinion (if not by the Kohl government) that Germans should fight alongside the coalition forces to liberate Kuwait; German participation was reduced to cheque-book diplomacy. When, soon after the war ended, Yugoslavia began its bloody disintegration, most sides (both within and outside Germany) still thought it would be inappropriate for Germany to become militarily involved. The awkward handling of the recognition of Croatia and Slovenia met with so much foreign criticism (including ample allegations that the Germans wanted to revive old fascist ties with the Croats) that Bonn thereafter opted for a low profile for several years.

But television reports of the developments, first along the Croat–Serb frontier, then in Bosnia, gradually weaned many German pacifists away from their earlier belief that all involvement in war is necessarily culpable. Before, the only publicly acceptable military action was seen by both parts of Germany as the defence of their own territory against aggression; all military action outside German territory was unthinkable (the reluctance of some German air force pilots to prepare for the defence of Germany's NATO partner Turkey in the Gulf war was the most infamous example). This has been changing gradually since 1992, however. Ronald Asmus with his RAND-sponsored polls, and Bernhard Fleckenstein and Hans-Georg Räder with the polls conducted for the German Armed Forces Institute for Social Research, have demonstrated that the proportion of Germans who believe their country should take a more active role in world politics (becoming 'more like Britain and France') has been growing, and had reached 62% by 1993.[32] By 1995, 75% of Germans asked were in favour of the participation of German troops 'in humanitarian missions and peacekeeping, or to prevent genocide, for defending threatened allies and for blocking proliferation of nuclear or chemical weapons'.[33] By the end of that year, even the Green Party (which had made its debut in German politics in the late 1970s and early 1980s over opposition to the Euromissile deployment) was reportedly edging away from its avowed opposition to such German military action alongside allies.[34]

While the political debate about German involvement alongside other foreign forces in peacekeeping and monitoring actions in Bosnia unfolded in 1993–4, it became apparent that the opposition parties in the Bundestag were more radically opposed to such involvement than the majority of public opinion. It thus reflected, rather than formed, public opinion when the Constitutional Court of the FRG ruled in June 1994 that such German military involvement was not unconstitutional, provided it was sanctioned by the UN or its principles and provided it had a majority in the federal parliament. Since then, the government has indeed managed to get the required majority vote to participate, first in NATO air strikes (July 1995)[35] and, since December 1995, in NATO's implementation force (IFOR) deployment designed to underpin the Dayton peace agreement for Bosnia. Indeed, since the Gulf war, Volker Rühe in the Ministry of Defence has embarked on a cautious programme of restructuring for the armed forces, aimed at creating professional units that could be employed alongside other allied forces in operations outside Germany. He and Helmut Kohl are thus carefully steering Germany towards assuming its role as team player in military as well as economic and political terms.

The slow awakening of German opinion to the military responsibilities the enlarged FRG might be expected to shoulder is often accompanied by exhortations from German and foreign commentators to Germany not to move too fast in this direction. There is little if any evidence, however, that the present German government, or indeed the present opposition, if it ever comes into government, would be tempted to abuse its military power. There is talk of the reduction of German military forces from the current 370,000 to perhaps 340,000.[36] The German Foreign Office seems to have learned its lesson about the dangers of unilateral action following its recognition of Croatia and Slovenia. The current government is sworn to multilateralism.[37] Yet large elements within the opposition parties, led by the Social Democrats, but also including the Greens, remain sworn to pacifism, and their leaders are even more cautious than the present government about any use of armed forces.[38]

Germany's security policy could thus be described as gradually 'maturing', as Ronald Asmus has put it.[39] The current and the previous US administrations seem to have recognized this, given their support for Germany as an equal actor among the Europeans and indeed in global dimensions. Even though there is little sign that UN Security Council membership will change in the near future,[40] the United States was among the first powers to support both the German and the Japanese candidacy for new permanent membership.[41]

Obviously, a variety of pitfalls could still lead to a renewed paralysis of the German government. These could range from revived sensitivities of Germany's neighbours through tactless handling of mainly domestic issues[42] to the need for Helmut Kohl's CDU-CSU to find a new coalition party to sustain his government. The junior coalition partner, the Free Democratic Party (FDP), has fought for its survival over the past few general elections even in west Germany alone, and may not survive the next one. On a local level, it has lost its seats in most *Länder* parliaments and thus governments, leaving the present Conservative-FDP coalition government in Bonn with a minority of representatives in the upper house, the Bundesrat. This could result in a change of the Conservatives' coalition, at the latest at the next general election.

The most likely candidate is the major opposition party SPD, now led by Oskar Lafontaine. The pacifist tendencies of its left wing could be of consequence in such a coalition, particularly when it comes to further crises and wars in which the UN and Germany's allies would like to see it participate in multinational action.[43] Nevertheless, developments in public opinion both inside and around Germany make it likely that Germany will in future be seen more often alongside other NATO allies in peacekeeping operations and possibly even active combat in such circumstances.

The SPD has also shown itself critical of the plan for a European Monetary Union, as one that would lead to too many sacrifices by a population which is feeling the cost of German unification. Perhaps the SPD is rediscovering the relatively harmless but stubborn nationalism of Kurt Schumacher, its first postwar leader.[44] While this would not necessarily spell disaster for Germany's neighbours, such a tendency, if the SPD were to come into government, would certainly not help European (let alone transatlantic) understanding and cooperation. Paradoxically, in the Federal Republic's political spectrum, it tends to be the conservative parties and the right wing of the SPD which are the most reliable and cooperative partners of the United States and the other Europeans. One of the SPD's leading defence specialists, who over time moved from the left to the right end of the party's spectrum, has most recently advocated the deepening of transatlantic relations by creating a 'civic' complement to NATO's military organization.[45]

In sum, Germany is developing slowly and haltingly into a major power both within Europe and beyond. Under the guidance of Kohl, Rühe and foreign minister Klaus Kinkel, it is aspiring to a permanent seat on the UNSC. It has often enough been told by other powers that this would carry certain obligations, including that of military force projection and military implementation of the UNSC's decisions. Germany's government is trying to give it the means of taking on such responsibilities, even if only on a conventional-force level. The military dimension of Germany's great-power status will always be less developed than that of Britain and France, let alone the USA and Russia: Germany has again voluntarily and irrevocably forsworn the production or possession of weapons of mass destruction.[46]

New missions for NATO

In the new security context, a new agenda has had to be formulated for an alliance which had hitherto been focused on one enemy, and a military organization which had planned almost exclusively the defence of the Treaty area against attacks from this one side. New questions were raised:

(1) Should NATO expand eastwards to integrate the former Soviet satellite states? Or should it concentrate on turning Russia into a security policy partner? This partnership might become impossible if NATO's borders approach the Russian homeland, reinforcing old Russian fears of Western aggressiveness.

(2) With the drive towards defence spending reductions in all member states, would NATO remain a credible military organization in any new or old role?

(3) What will NATO's future mission(s) be? Merely to hedge against a revived Russian threat? Or should it take on missions on behalf of the UN or the CSCE/OSCE in areas not covered by Article 5 of the North Atlantic Treaty?

The answers to all three questions are interdependent and the Alliance for several years seemed trapped in its inability to calculate all variables simultaneously.

Enlargement

From its very inception, the North Atlantic Treaty provided scope for enlargement on the European continent. The issue of new membership in Eastern Europe was firmly on the agenda by 1991, when political insecurity in Moscow led to fears for the independence of the USSR's former satellites. In mid-1991, NATO signalled its concern for their security and stability: 'Our own security is inseparably linked to that of all other states in Europe. The consolidation and preservation throughout the continent of democratic societies and their freedom from any form of coercion or intimidation are therefore of direct and material concern to us.'[47]

This was reiterated during the August 1991 crisis in Moscow: 'Noting the enhanced concern of Central and Eastern European states, we reiterate our conviction that our own security is inseparably linked to that of all other states in Europe, particularly to that of the emerging democracies. We expect the Soviet Union to respect the integrity and security of all states in Europe.'[48]

But both the Bush administration and the German government felt that this was not enough. Foreign Minister Hans-Dietrich Genscher and his ministry secured US agreement to a joint German–US proposal for the creation of the North Atlantic Cooperation Council (NACC), published on 2 October 1991. It provided for the creation of a forum by which all former Warsaw Pact members (including Russia) could jointly consult with NATO at regular multilateral meetings.[49]

While this was welcomed by the leaders of Czechoslovakia (Havel), Hungary (Antall) and Poland (Walesa) a few days later, they hinted that the creation of NACC was not enough.[50] At the NATO summit in Rome in early November 1991, President Bush raised East European hopes that membership of NACC meant admission to the ante-chamber, which would 'in the long run' lead to full membership of NATO.[51]

There are two main reasons why NACC was seen as inadequate by central and east Europeans: it does not give them a security guarantee; and it includes them in the same forum as the Russians, making it impossible for them to talk to NATO members other than in the presence of the Russians, against whom they wanted Western assurance. Consistent pressure and statements of dissatisfaction produced a new compromise: Partnership for Peace (PfP), a treaty offered to every former

Warsaw Pact state (and also the former neutrals), to be concluded by each of them bilaterally with NATO as a whole.[52] In this way, all of them could be treated similarly (nobody was excluded except by their own choice), while being treated differently. This enabled NATO to create different relations with different countries, including giving them advice on military and security matters, joint exercises, and establishing contacts with them individually, without extending NATO membership or security guarantees, and without offending Russia by excluding it.

Ever since, we have witnessed a diplomatic ballet with three constantly repeated movements: the North Atlantic Council, or an American leader, or the German Minister of Defence, begins with a dramatic pirouette stating that NATO will expand (when and to include whom being left open), upon which a Russian leader shows with a *grand chassé* that this is unacceptable, would be seen as offensive and would lead to severe countermeasures. Finally come the petits battements of the leaders of Central European states, pleading for full admission to NATO, pointing to the hostility of the Russian response as an argument for their need for more than just NACC and PfP. The chorus of old European NATO members provides constant background movement with anxious *changements de pieds*, stating that they would not welcome NATO expansion after all as it would unnecessarily antagonize the Russians, import central-east European regional problems into NATO, and spoil the old family feeling in the alliance.

The odd result of this is that NATO as a whole, but also the Bush and Clinton administrations and indeed the German government, have all repeatedly committed themselves to NATO expansion, most recently in September 1995 with the Enlargement Study,[53] and yet it is strongly contested as long as there is no major crisis in Russia.

Even within individual NATO states, reactions have been strikingly different (leaving aside the shared fear of angering the Russians into becoming implacable enemies of NATO once again). To the universalists, the creation of democracies in central and eastern Europe, however unstable they might be at present, logically leads to their inclusion in the community of values of the North Atlantic nations.[54] To others, new members would undermine the identity and cohesion of the North Atlantic nations as a 'community of fate' brought together by the shared Cold War experience. On the European side, there is also a jealous wish to keep their special relationships with the United States to themselves.[55]

Nobody so far seems to have worked out a coherent and convincing solution to a series of related problems, such as what is to be done to enhance the security of countries such as the Baltic states or even Ukraine, unlikely to be admitted to NATO, and how the creation of 'different zones of security', new dividing lines, new spheres of influence can be avoided.

Meanwhile, the focus of NATO's attention has thankfully shifted from the abstract issue of membership to practical measures designed to help central and east European countries restructure their armed forces and defence industries, firmly plant a culture of civilian control of the military, restructure their defence ministries accordingly, and acquaint themselves with NATO standards and procedure. The association of forces from individual central and east European countries with forces from NATO countries in individual military operations (mainly in the former Yugoslavia) is also going some way to consolidate democratic structures and procedures. Parallel developments are under way between the Western European Union (WEU) members and their new Associate Partners in eastern (central) Europe. Such cooperation, along with economic advice, exchanges and scholarships, is bringing these countries closer to the North Atlantic nations than any declarations would do at present.

Force cuts and reconfiguration

With the disintegration of its former main enemy, it became clear that NATO's old military structure was in need of reform. The layer-cake structure of its integrated military forces made little sense once the inner German border had disappeared and once Russia no longer controlled Poland, Hungary, Czechoslovakia, Romania and Bulgaria. Therefore, since 1991 a reform of NATO's military structure has been undertaken.[56]

Soon NATO reforms became a race against unilateral national force reductions by its members (see Table 4.5). The US reduced its forces in Europe from 325,000 in the late 1980s to 187,000 in March 1993, announcing a reduction to 100,000 by 1996.[57] By August 1993, there was talk of further cuts, to 65,000 troops,[58] until the Bottom-Up Review fixed the level at 100,000 until the year 2000.[59] This, as we shall see, challenged a fundamental assumption of NATO's military and command structure: that the US would provide the leadership as it provided most of the strategic capability, and one of the largest forces in Europe (the largest overall in the NATO area). This led even Americanophile Europeans to speculate that the United States might withdraw its forces totally, abandoning Europe to its fate.[60]

As early as 1991, Canada announced substantial force reductions in Europe (from 6,600 in 1991 to 1,100 by the end of 1995) and in 1992 it

Table 4.4: Force cuts of NATO members after the end of the Cold War

All armed forces:	1989	1995	Projected
Belgium	88,300	47,200	40,000
Canada (total)	90,100	70,500	
of which in Europe	7,100	none permanently	
Denmark	29,300	33,100	
France	456,900	409,000	
Germany	488,700	339,900	
Greece	214,000	171,300	
Italy	386,000	328,700	
Netherlands	74,400		
Norway	35,800	30,000	
Portugal	73,900	54,200	
Spain	309,500	209,000	
Turkey	635,300	507,800	
United Kingdom	316,700	236,900	
USA (total)	2,163,200	1,547,300	
of which in Europe	317,000	139,200	100,000

Sources: IISS: *Military Balance 1988/89* (London: Brasseys, 1988) and *Military Balance 1995/96* (London: Oxford University Press, 1995).

declared that it would withdraw its forces totally.[61] It thus deprived itself of much leverage in subsequent military discussions with allies. Canada then decided to deploy those forces in the former Yugoslavia, so they remained in Europe, albeit with a modified mission. Unfortunately this received comparatively little press coverage.[62]

Belgium announced in January 1993 a reduction of its army from 80,000 to 40,000, along with the abolition of conscription.[63] France announced the abandonment of conscription in 1996.

NATO announced in 1993 that its overall forces were to be cut by 25% by 1997. These would be reconfigured into, first, the main defence forces, that is multinational and national formations stationed in Europe, at varying (but mainly low) levels of readiness. Second, there would be reaction forces, highly mobile multinational ground, air and maritime forces, which would be kept at a higher level of readiness. The reaction forces themselves would consist of Immediate Reaction Forces and the Allied Forces Central Europe (ACE) Rapid Reaction Corps. Third, there would be augmentation forces, apart from national reserves, essentially the US and Canadian forces on the other side of the Atlantic.[64]

The cuts were clearly budget-driven in all the countries affected, but the reduced budgets also reflected the perception that the Cold War levels of defence spending were simply not needed any longer. Whatever efforts were made to reduce force levels without sacrificing force effectiveness, the retention of conscription by Germany, Portugal, Italy, Greece and Turkey means a reduction in the length of military service, and thus, in the eyes of most military experts, in the effectiveness of the conscript forces. The reconfigurations into different multinational units has often been driven by political considerations, which again has meant the danger of reduced military effectiveness while problems of logistics and standardization are sorted out.

It is thus by no means clear what sort of military operations these NATO-assigned forces are capable of at short notice, and NATO's long-term study of command structure, designed to enable the organization to do more with fewer forces, is not yet completed.[65] The question of how much can actually be done arises even for the largest of the NATO member states, the US, with its considerably down-scaled military (now at 71.5% of its latest Cold War strength).

The first military review, presented at the beginning of the Clinton administration, postulated only the ability to fight and win two medium-sized wars, one after the other (and neither in Europe): in the first, victory would be achieved; the second enemy would be held, then defeated ('win-hold-win').[66] Clinton's first Secretary of Defence, Les Aspin, opposed this as too limited a capability, which would dangerously expose the US to the danger of a double defeat.[67] The Bottom-Up Review finally opted for what was estimated to be a 'win-win' capability, in which two medium-sized wars could be fought and won simultaneously.[68] It is important to note that this implies some reliance by the United States on its European allies. As Warren Christopher and William Perry phrased it, 'By mobilizing the support of other nations and leveraging our resources through alliances and institutions, we can achieve important objectives without asking American soldiers to bear all the risks, or American taxpayers to pay all the bills. That is a sensible bargain that the American people support.'[69]

Another Bottom-up Review of US defence policy is expected in 1997, after the presidential elections.[70] By then, it should be clearer how successful NATO's new post-Cold War and post-Gulf war structure has been in tackling the very limited task of securing peace in Bosnia.

Missions: out of area or out of business[71]

The earliest and simplest post-Cold War consensus among the North Atlantic nations concerned the continuing importance of NATO as a safety-net, in case the nuclear giant Russia should revert to its bad old expansionist ways. But was there scope for additional missions? Both the Gulf war and the Yugoslav war indicated that more limited conflicts were still occurring, even within Europe. Ironically, since 1948 France had sought agreement among the three North Atlantic powers on issues arising in areas outside the North Atlantic Treaty area.[72] The limitations of the area to which the North Atlantic Treaty was to apply had been inserted at the wish of the Americans, who, at the time the Treaty was drafted, feared becoming involved in the colonial problems of France and Britain. In 1958, de Gaulle made France's continued cooperation in NATO conditional on the creation of such a three-power directorate to establish a concerted policy on issues throughout the world. As the United States did not grant his wish, de Gaulle gradually withdrew French forces from NATO's integrated military structure, a process completed by the end of 1967.[73] Meanwhile the Americans had to bear the consequences of their inability to enlist European support for their policies in Southeast Asia.

The issue of harmonization beyond the geographical limits to which the Treaty applied never quite went away. But the Gulf war brought it into focus at the end of 1990 by highlighting the absence of any mechanism for agreement and hence consensus between the US, Britain and France, the most important among the powers that fought in the coalition against Iraq. At the same time, it became clear that the NATO members which joined the anti-Iraq coalition were using forces usually assigned to NATO, and NATO assets in the Gulf, benefiting from the experience of NATO joint exercises and planning. Yet they still thought that they could not undertake this action in their NATO capacity, on account of the regional limitations (Article 6) of Article 5 of the North Atlantic Treaty, according to which an attack on one would be regarded as an attack on all.

The question was raised why this regional limitation should apply to actions undertaken by NATO which did not come under Article 5, provided they had the blessing of the UN or the OSCE. By 1992, Secretary-General Manfred Wörner had made himself the advocate of such 'out-of-area' missions. The specific areas in which NATO envisaged involvement were Nagorny Karabakh and Yugoslavia.[74]

France, however, was not keen on this widening of NATO's competence, as its government repeatedly made clear. The French government apparently feared that the United States wanted to reap the publicity benefit from peacekeeping operations in Yugoslavia, without itself deploying ground forces there, while France and Britain would risk casualties.[75] Indeed, earliest NATO involvement was very limited, and was only gradually extended to cover diverse missions.[76] Yet at the end of 1992, Germany and Italy (in view of vivid memories of their policies in the area during the Second World War), the US, Portugal, Greece and Turkey were still unwilling to contribute to force deployments.[77] This was an early hint of the pattern explained above, namely action by alliances of the willing, while others among the North Atlantic nations would stand aside to give, at best, lukewarm rhetorical support.

Disagreement among the North Atlantic nations over the future of their relationship was fought out on the backs of the victims of war among the south Slavs. As the war shifted from Croatia and Slovenia to Bosnia, Germany withdrew from prominence in the Balkans, while the US favoured policies radically opposed to those of the French and British governments. Repeatedly, the US advocated air strikes against forces that could be identified as aggressors, but consistently until the end of 1995 refused to deploy ground forces in what it saw as another Vietnam quagmire. The French and the British, however, who deployed troops in the former Yugoslavia to ensure the supply of basic commodities to the civilian populations in various besieged towns, were opposed to air strikes. They feared that their own forces might be taken hostage in revenge, and saw the US alternative as an escalation of the war.[78]

None of the peace agreements which the Europeans attempted to negotiate between the warring parties was respected. The Europeans, particularly the French who initially had hoped that the Yugoslav war would prove that Europe could sort out minor wars without US help, began to see the need for US forces as additional guarantors of any peace agreement. The French, in a spectacular turnabout (which secured them the position of privileged interlocutor of the United States in Europe), solicited US involvement in the conflict.[79]

It still took another year-and-a-half before a solution was hammered out that brought peace to Bosnia and saved NATO. For the failure to reach agreement between the three Atlantic great powers was seen to put serious strains on the alliance – the greatest since Suez, as one observer commented.[80] The Dayton peace agreement of November 1995 and the constitution of the multinational IFOR sent out to enforce it were celebrated as a great breakthrough – for peace in Bosnia, but also for the survival of NATO and the resumption of US leadership.[81]

The crucible of the Balkans led to a number of other results and lessons. Over several years (1992–5), the policies of NATO members towards the former Yugoslavia confirmed the emerging tendency of military missions to take the form of operations by a select group of countries willing to shoulder them, even though the operation was agreed by NATO as a whole.

The Yugoslav war showed that even in contingencies of low intensity affecting primarily the Europeans (not the North Americans), the Europeans continue to rely heavily on the United States. Certainly, having soldiers from other parts of the world involved in peacekeeping and peace-making in the former Yugoslavia is an important gesture, underpinning UN-bestowed legitimacy. But given how directly (or indirectly) the Balkan war concerned NATO members on the two sides of the Atlantic, a European power or the Europeans collectively through the EU or WEU might have been expected to take the lead in imposing peace. Instead, they decided once again to seek US leadership. This bodes ill for the Europeans' ability to keep their own continent in order.

Interpretations differ as to whether it was the approaching US presidential election campaign which pushed the administration into belatedly shouldering this burden, or whether the US lead in the Bosnian peace deal at the end of 1995 was a sign of a new US commitment to being a global policeman.[82] Much will depend on the distribution of power and views in Washington after the presidential elections.

With France's decision once again to become a major player within NATO, Combined Joint Task Forces (CJTFs) will clearly become important. The concept of the CJTF was devised from the end of 1993 in response to French refusals to assign forces directly to NATO command structures.[83] Under this formula, the national forces usually assigned to NATO would for the purpose of a CJTF operation be 'separable' from the NATO military command, but would not be assigned to the WEU permanently (and would thus not be seen as 'separate' from NATO).[84] Devised to facilitate the deployment of French forces in the context of the Yugoslav war, the command structures and distribution of command posts within CJTFs have become major political issues, particularly between the French and the US. Both countries are notoriously reluctant to subordinate their own forces to foreign commanders, for historical reasons, but also out of pride. Purportedly, the issue was resolved with the North Atlantic Council meeting in Berlin in June 1996.[85]

To conclude, then, the decisive differences between 'out-of-area' operations and Article 5 operations are the entirely voluntary nature of individual NATO members' contributions to the mission,[86] the need for a consensus to form within NATO that NATO assets can be used for the mission, and the formal need for UN or OSCE sanctioning.[87]

The aforementioned dichotomy between the search for legitimacy and *ad hoc* great-power cooperation on individual issues is clear here: if the Americans, British and French agree that they want to act together, and persuade the UNSC (of which they are permanent members) to bless their action, they will do so. If they need more than their national assets, namely also NATO assets, they will ask for NATO as a whole to approve this action. Nevertheless, NATO as a whole will hardly be activated. Not every member of NATO is likely to send forces to support the operation. *De facto*, NATO, or any CJTF arrangement, is a label which can be attached to an operation conducted by the three Atlantic great powers, with token or symbolic cooperation from a few other NATO members, and assorted parties outside NATO.

Two such parties assume a particular importance. In order to secure the blessing of the UNSC, it is highly important that neither Russia nor China should feel that its interests are harmed by the operation. Particularly for an operation in Europe or the Middle East, it is crucial for the Atlantic great powers to coax Russia into cooperation. In the IFOR peacekeeping operation in Bosnia, it is thus infinitely more important for the US, Britain and France to have Russian cooperation (or at least benevolence) than to have the active support of NATO members such as Italy, Greece, Turkey, Spain, Portugal, Denmark, Iceland or Norway. The emerging pattern is thus not one of NATO going 'out of area', but of the Atlantic great powers drawing on their own national and NATO assets to undertake the operation. They will use NATO, but they will depend more crucially on the support of Russia (and the non-opposition of China).

The question remains what the Europeans will be prepared to do in minor contingencies on their own. And beyond that, what are the Europeans prepared to do for the Americans? Since the 1960s, the Europeans have done very little to stand by the North Americans in dealing with Asian security. Leaving aside the fruitless discussion about the justification of the Vietnam war, Europeans have on the whole shown little understanding for US concerns about China and, concomitantly, the relationships among its Far Eastern neighbours. Convinced that their continent would be the prime theatre of war, Europeans rarely (as for example during the Cuban missile crisis) thought much about their own reciprocal commitment to the defence of North America. And after the Korean war, with the progressive withdrawal from former colonies,

European countries rarely took an active security interest in the Far East. The last important exception, Britain's interest in Hong Kong, will come to an end with the assumption of Chinese control in 1997.

In both questions of security and trade developments, Europeans have remained aloof from American policies towards the Far East. Although it is clear to Europeans and North Americans alike that East and Southeast Asia comprise both important economic competitors and important potential markets, Europeans have given disproportionately little attention to this area. Although optimists see signs that this is changing, it remains unclear whether military instruments such as the Allied Reaction Force will be used beyond Europe and the African arc of crisis on its southern rim. This is reflected also by the very select nature of the few 'joint actions' upon which the Europeans have hitherto embarked. This is in the context of what was supposed to be a 'Common Foreign and Security Policy' but amounts to little more than a select list of issues which are so non-controversial that consensus on them is possible.[88]

The question of reciprocity is something that any sensible US government will bring to the attention of the Europeans. It is time that the Europeans stopped behaving as net receivers of security, taking action only where their own interest is directly concerned. Any new transatlantic bargain should compel the Europeans to back the North Americans in their attempts to protect military stability in the Far East and elsewhere in the world. Given the EU's gross economic product compared with that of the United States, there is no excuse for European passivity. That military matters remain a purely national prerogative and that, among the Europeans, the United States can only draw on the support of the two medium-sized powers, Britain and France, in these matters are factors working against US interests and indeed international stability. It would be in the greater interest of all sides if Europe's potential could be more effectively tapped through further political and military integration, and through the association of non-EU or non-WEU powers on an *ad hoc* basis. As national forces, Belgian, Danish, Norwegian or Portuguese units are barely relevant. As standardized units of European armed forces they would collectively matter:[89] this is the simple explanation of why Europe has such an impressive number of forces and equipment, and yet cannot even provide the forces to pacify one of the smaller states of what used to be Yugoslavia without the US stepping in. Further integration of foreign, security and defence policy of the EU will not happen in 1996, and a European army will not develop beyond the symbolic gestures of the Eurocorps and the Franco-Italo-Spanish EUROFOR.

Chapter 5

The Age of Mercury

'It's the economy, stupid!'– purportedly the leitmotif
of Clinton's 1992 election campaign

The fear of major war having receded, Mars, though still asserting himself in bloody local wars and terrorism, is all but eclipsed by Mercury ascendant. Economics have always been a major factor in transatlantic relations, but they seem now to have assumed a role unprecedented since the Wall Street Crash of 1929 and the resulting world economic crisis. But there are some additional factors, such as the erosion of the state's power over its own economy. The rise of multinationals, empires of production and commerce, and the increase in international investment have created centres of power that cannot be controlled and can barely be checked by the governments of individual states.[1] Meanwhile, unemployment, social welfare bills and national budget deficits are growing on both sides of the Atlantic, where populations are ageing and traditional patterns of social support have all but disappeared. While the national budgets of the EU members and Canada are directly burdened with the price of welfare for all, the indirect costs of social welfare to the US GNP are also considerable in terms of labour costs.

We shall consider below the particularly important effects of the recession on US behaviour in the international arena. The aggravation of Canada's Quebec identity crisis by high unemployment has been mentioned above. The recession has led to domestic crises in France, Spain and Italy, and to a lesser extent in Britain. Economic issues have risen in importance here, too, and it is questionable whether a significant number of countries can meet the criteria for Economic and Monetary Union by the end of the century. While there are still firm believers in the economic

74

benefits of monetary union, it is admitted by many Germans (including Chancellor Kohl himself[2]) that the main motivation behind it is political, the common currency being a means to make integration and joint policy irreversible. But individual governments' attempts to meet the challenging criteria are at least a factor complicating their policies to overcome the recession.

These difficulties became particularly visible in France during the wave of strikes which paralysed the country in December 1995. But the phenomenon of the *fracture sociale* – ever lower voting participation and, for the first time in the France's Fifth Republic, a president who in the second round was elected by less than an absolute majority of French voters; the high level of long-term unemployment, the tendency of an underclass within society to be permanently excluded from the economic cycle through unemployment – can be found in Britain and other North Atlantic countries as well. Governments will be very preoccupied with finding ways to alleviate the economic crisis. This will not necessarily have a negative effect upon their willingness to pursue active policies on issues of international security, but keeping costs down will be a major consideration. Willingness to become involved in issues that are of less than direct concern to a given country will always depend on the success and cost of previous operations.

The effects of the recession troubling Europe and North America since 1989 are difficult to treat by individual governments separately.

Table 5.1: The unemployed as a percentage of the workforce

Spain	22.2	United Kingdom	8.6
Finland	17.0	New Zealand	8.3*
Ireland	14.6	Portugal	7.3
France	11.6	The Netherlands	6.7
Italy	12.6	Denmark	6.1
Canada	10.5*	USA	6.1
Belgium	10.3	Norway	5.5*
Australia	9.7*	Austria	5.5*
Greece	9.7*	Switzerland	4.7*
Sweden	9.7	Japan	2.9*
Germany	8.7	European Union	10.9

Sources: Figures date from December 1995 (November 1995 for the Netherlands), and are taken from 'L'aggravation du chômage se poursuit dans la plupart des pays européens', *Le Monde*, 10 February, 1996; except for figures marked *, which are 1994 annual average taken from Mario v. Baratta (ed). *Der Fischer Weltalmanach '96* (Frankfurt/Main: Fischer Taschenbuch Verlag, 1995), p. 947.

But does that mean that concerted action by several trading partners will provide the best answer? Or *dirigisme*, centralized state intervention, or regional cooperation in Europe alone? Theories of economic relations and the effects of government policies on markets, production figures, employment, etc. cannot be predicted with scientific certainty by any school. This is crucial when it comes to identifying, let alone prescribing policies for, the economic problems facing the countries on both sides of the Atlantic and other parts of the world.

The fact remains that the recession is an international phenomenon and has affected primarily the members of the EU, but also Canada and the United States (see Table 5.1).

The United States: economic crisis and the erosion of central power

Under the confluence of two major factors, US attitudes towards the rest of the world have undergone a significant change since 1990. The two factors are the end of the Cold War and the recession. Together they have changed the order of US priorities from external to domestic and economic.

Centripetal and centrifugal forces

Since the American Revolution the nation's political culture has been torn in two different directions by a centralizing, federalist tendency on the one hand and a decentralizing, even anarchic tendency on the other.[3] The federal government with its monopoly of foreign policy and defence is the expression of the former; the jealously defended autonomy in many other areas of government enjoyed by the individual federal states reflects the latter. The US has long been the home of strong anti-federal or even anarchic movements, of which the latest radical examples are the militia movements, and small anarchist groups protesting their civic rights to deny state control of their private financial and legal transactions.[4] (These also in part explain current rumblings within the US that are highly critical of the United Nations and its role in interstate relations.) While these anarchic groups are insignificant minorities, the causes for which they are fighting – the right to carry arms, the right to defy any state intervention in or control of their private lives – are dear to the hearts of many Americans, ideals that can be traced back to the independence from state control sought by the Pilgrim Fathers as much as by the anti-federalists who opposed the constitution of the Union in 1787.

But the balance between integration and decentralization is also anchored in the US constitution itself. Within the federal government, the Congress (and within it particularly the Senate, representing the federal states) is designed to check the power concentrated in the hands of the executive (or administration), headed by the US president. During the Cold War, the pressure of a strongly perceived external threat to US national security shifted the balance between states and federal government, between Congress and president, in favour of Washington and, within Washington, in favour of the presidency and its executive agencies. In persuading Congress annually that the United States had to foot a defence bill higher not only in absolute terms, but also in GNP and per capita terms, than that of any other NATO member, the administration received very substantial powers and scope for action in its security policy.

This is not to claim that the Cold War years saw a US administration acting independently from, or unchallenged by, Congress. Many instances can be recalled – from the McMahon Act of 1947 eliminating the administration's freedom to share nuclear technology, to the Fulbright and Mansfield campaigns for the reduction of US troops in Europe in the 1960s and 1970s, to the War Powers Act of 1973 limiting the period for which the president can authorize the use of forces abroad – where Congress more or less successfully countered presidential policy.[5] But despite these very important examples of Congressional policy initiatives, the administration tended to have a stronger position during the Cold War, a strength that fed on Soviet and Warsaw Pact forces and nuclear arsenals, on Soviet covert operations and Chinese subversive interventions in less developed countries.

This balance has shifted in the opposite direction since the end of the Cold War. One could point more specifically to the beginning of Bill Clinton's Democrat presidency in 1993, and again more precisely to the return of a Republican-dominated Congress at the end of 1994. The bill introduced by Congress in early 1995 aiming at limiting the administration's ability to conduct defence policy is most symptomatic of the tug-of-war between Congress and presidency in the post-Cold War environment.

The rise of domestic issues
Bill Clinton won the presidential elections of 1992 with a clear mandate to pay more attention to domestic issues and the state of the US economy, in an international context where the American public was no longer convinced that its national security was substantially threatened from the outside. Thus it was mainly by choice that Clinton reduced the importance accorded to non-economic foreign policy and military issues. On domestic issues, however, the tug-of-war over the responsibilities of the federal

government as opposed to state governments has to be resolved from case to case, as issues such as economic development (other than foreign trade) and subsidies, social welfare and benefits, and many areas of legislation are seen as prerogatives of the individual states' governments. Inevitably, the administration has come up against greater institutional opposition to its policies, opposition that is a function of competing structures at least as much as it concerns differences on policy aims or implementation.

The return of a Republican-dominated Congress during the mid-term elections of 1994 has also led to greater institutional rivalry. House Speaker Newt Gingrich has been consistently obstructing the administration's initiatives on a host of issues not limited to defence and security. Indeed, the Republican elements in Congress have at times resisted defence cuts.[6] The Republican presidential candidate Robert Dole, in particular, urged the administration to adopt a more interventionist policy in Bosnia.[7] Policy initiatives do not lie solely with the administration: indeed, sometimes European leaders feel that they have to deal with Congressional leaders directly, rather than with the administration, when bargaining about joint policy.[8]

All sides agree, however, on the need to counter the effects of the recession affecting the United States since 1991. It has had particularly painful effects on a labour force which is not comprehensively protected against high unemployment rates through an extensive, state-run social security system as in Europe or Canada. Since 1992, the performance of the US economy and unemployment figures have become the top consideration for the great majority of Americans, including the governing elites. The notable decline of interest in foreign and security matters (where they do not touch directly on economic issues) has since 1993 led to repeated disappointment among America's European friends, who find no interlocutors in Washington[9] nor travelling Congresspeople who make it beyond, at best, London.[10]

In public opinion polls conducted in the United States in autumn 1994, respondents were asked to cite a 'very important' foreign policy goal of the US.[11] The highest-ranking issues in 1994 tended to be those affecting the US social and economic situation itself. Second highest came military threats to the US. The traditional idealistic missions – humanitarian, democratizing, protection of the weak – came relatively low down on the list, with a significant drop since 1990.

US public opinion has never in the last two decades been more than lukewarm in its support for foreign economic aid. But public (as opposed to foreign policy-making and specialist elite) opinion is now uniformly in favour of cutting existing aid budgets for Eastern Europe and Russia, Africa, Latin America and the Middle East.[13] Interestingly, also, both public and elite opinion has since around 1980 favoured (and favoured increasingly) a *reduction* of US commitment to NATO (with an all-time low in 1990).[12]

Thus the waning of what interest there has ever been in foreign affairs among the US public went along with a surge in the feeling that it was time the United States stopped subsidizing security (and thus, indirectly, economic prosperity) in other parts of the world and that it was time it adopted a more active, self-interested economic policy towards foreign markets. The protection of US values *at home* has come to be seen as more important, and increasingly more threatened, than the projection of these values abroad: a shift from universalism to a defensive retrenchment after a long period of perceived overextension. Since 1992, successive US governments have exerted pressure on the Europeans to make concessions on trade negotiations by linking them with US support for NATO.[13] As President Clinton's trade representative told the European Commission in Brussels in March 1993, 'The days when we could afford to subordinate our economic interests to foreign policy or defence concerns are long past'.[14]

We thus see a transformation of US public opinion about the country's role in world affairs and the degree of readiness it should show to make major sacrifices for the benefit of other countries or indeed the world order in general (see Table 5.2). Even at the height of the Cold War, it was said to be difficult to obtain enthusiastic support for US foreign and military policies from the largely inward-looking populations of the Midwest. Since the end of the Cold War, it has clearly become more difficult still.

By contrast, a sense of economic rivalry with other powers – which in itself is as old as the United States – is in some ways now dominating the universalist, idealist streaks in the US attitude towards the rest of the world. The strength with which this is felt is clearly reflected in the emphasis put on economic relations by the Clinton administration right from the start, not least in its dealings with the Europeans.[15] It pervaded the rather uncompromising attitude adopted by the US in the final stages of the Uruguay Round of the General Agreement on Tariffs and Trade (GATT) negotiations which concluded in 1994, and it was a pronounced feature of US–Japanese relations even before Bill Clinton moved into the White House.

Table 5.2: Question: 'Which federal government programs should be expanded, cut back or remain the same?'

	1978	1982	1986	1990	1994
Aid to education	+47	+52	+65	+71	+71
Combat illegal drugs				+66	
Combat violence & crime					+75
Social security		+43	+56	+52	+42
Space programme			+7	-15	-13
Welfare & relief programmes	-30	-4	+10	+16	+64*
Defence	+10	-10	-12	-29	-13
Aid to other nations:					
Economic	-39	-46	-37	-54	-49
Military	-59	-60	-58	-68	-64

*Termed health care in 1994.
Note: The figures are derived by subtracting the percentage that wants to cut back funding for a specific programme from the percentage that wants to expand it.
Sources: John E. Reilly (ed.), *American Public Opinion and U.S. Foreign Policy 1991* (Chicago: Chicago Council on Foreign Relations, 1991), p. 11; John E. Reilly (ed.), *American Public Opinion and U.S. Foreign Policy 1995* (Chicago: Chicago Council on Foreign Relations, 1995), p. 12.

With Americans focused in this way on economic affairs, the present incumbent of the White House, and probably his successor, must see their mandate as one of promoting US economic performance through trade. This means, for the US, that it has a choice between fierce competition and, if solutions can be found that are to the mutual benefit of both the United States and its trading partners, cooperation. The quest for cooperation through a reduction or removal of tariffs is rooted in the doctrinaire belief of the United States in the beneficial effects of free trade which goes back to the Boston Tea Party at least (but all sides in this agreement have insisted on the preservation of protective tariffs in certain areas). This belief is reflected in the United States' long leadership in the GATT negotiations and most recently in its support for the creation of the World Trade Organization (WTO). It has led to the conclusion of the Free Trade Agreement (FTA) with Canada in 1989, widened in 1994 to become NAFTA including Mexico. Most recently, Bill Clinton has been pursuing better economic relations with the Far East through the Asia-Pacific Economic Cooperation agreement (APEC). Although initiatives aimed more specifically at bringing down trade barriers between NAFTA and the EU have come from Canada and some Europeans rather than from the United States, there seems to be substantial interest there, too, in such a mutually beneficial solution that could turn competition into cooperation.

US foreign policy, then, is dominated by economic issues as a function of its domestic concerns. As long as no major military threat arises in the world, this is not likely to change: US policy will continue to be dominated not by some abstract sense of isolationism, but by its domestic, and particularly its economic, agenda. Consequently, trade issues will top the agenda of any transatlantic relations.

Trade

NAFTA: extended to Europe?

Is it possible at the turn of the millennium for the Europeans and the North Americans to solve their in many respects similar economic problems through cooperation, or will they turn to rivalry? According to 1995 figures of the European Commission, the United States is the EU countries' largest external trading partner, absorbing 20% of US exports and producing 18% of US imports; just under 17% of EU imports come from the US, and 18% of its exports flow there. Moreover, the EU provides 53% of total foreign direct investment in the US; the US in turn provides 42% of foreign direct investment in the EU.[16] The EU is, after Canada and Japan, the third largest import source for the United States at US$111 billion per annum, and its second largest export market with US$100 billion, second only to Canada and before Japan.[17] Economic links between the two sides of the Atlantic are thus significant, and there is competition for exports from both NAFTA and the EU.

While a call for a new transatlantic charter has been made several times in the history of NATO, a significant feature of this latest wave is that it is focusing increasingly on economic issues. In themselves, proposals for closer cooperation between the United States and Europe on economic issues are nothing new; they go back to the early post-Second World War era. But the new international environment, and the particular emphasis put by the United States on trade, have given the economic dimension of transatlantic relations an added importance. The acrimonious prolongation of the Uruguay Round (originally expected to be completed by 1990, but then delayed until 1994) spelled out this lesson on both sides of the Atlantic.

As early as 14 December 1989, Secretary of State James Baker called for cooperation between the US and the EC, with 'a significantly strength-ened set of institutional and consultative links'.[18] In spring 1993 the US ambassador to the European Union proposed a series of measures be-yond the conclusion of the GATT round, listing competition policy, the removal of regulatory barriers, and a further opening of services markets. This he described as one item on a broader 'Agenda for a Euro-Atlantic Community'.[19] This is not far from the ideas sketched by French Defence Minister Léotard in his article of 30 September 1994: he described the objective of the new Atlantic partnership he was proposing as 'in due course, the realization of a free trade zone'.[20] By January 1995, Secretary of State Warren Christopher added his voice to those advocating the advancement of 'the most open global trading system in history' as the first priority of US foreign policy.[21] Robert Dole also expressed his support for closer economic relationships with Europe.

The call for a transatlantic free trade area (TAFTA) and a new transatlantic treaty was taken up by Sir Leon Brittan, vice-president of the European Commission, in April 1995. In the following months, the Commission was charged to work out the feasibility of a TAFTA.[22]

On the European continent, the German Foreign Minister, Klaus Kinkel, took up the call for a transatlantic free market in his speech at the Wehrkunde conference on 5 February 1995.[23] In May 1995, the Canadian Minister for International Trade, Roy MacLaren, added his voice to those of the Europeans, emphasizing his government's interest in a free trade area including all of the NAFTA region and the EU.[24] There is clearly some concern in Canada not to become one of the 'spokes' of a 'hub-and-spokes' system of transatlantic trade centred on the United States. This concern already existed at the creation of NAFTA, which Canada in-sisted had to be a triangular relationship between Canada, the US and Mexico, allowing direct trade between Canada and Mexico without going through the US. Since then, Canada has actively pursued this plan.[25]

Given the relatively positive experience Canada has had with its Free Trade Agreement with the US,[26] many experts seem convinced that all sides have more to gain than to lose from working towards TAFTA. They are equally convinced, however, that such an agreement cannot be achieved overnight. For believers in free trade and the benefits of ra-tionalization of enterprises on an international scale, TAFTA could ulti-mately stimulate the world economy as a whole, and the Far Eastern industrialized countries could be interested in membership.

Nevertheless, tariffs protecting individual NAFTA countries and the

EU as a whole are relatively low even now. Proponents of the creation of a transatlantic free trade area see mutual benefit in their total elimination, and indeed in the elimination of non-tariff barriers to trade. If this is on balance really in the interest of all the North Atlantic producers, it would be worth pursuing, even though harmonizing the different sets of rules and standards would be a time-consuming task. But the effects would probably not be significant. Canada, the United States and the EU members, all of them members of the WTO, have nevertheless agreed to work for this long-term aim. Any substantial change in the near future is no more likely to be approved by Congress than it is to be attractive to the French farming lobby. The Joint Action Plan put out by the EU and the US at their summit in Madrid on 3 December 1995 commissioned a joint study about progress in this area, but it would be overly optimistic to expect early results. The interest of such steps lies in prospects for European–North American agreement beyond the North Atlantic area.

Global trade patterns
The patterns of trade in the world economy as it has developed over the past few decades are substantially different from the equally global trading patterns in previous history. For centuries, industries in Europe depended on imports of raw materials from far-away continents and on exports of finished products to recipients in equally remote areas. The possession of colonies seemed profitable to industrialists and merchants in Britain, France, the Netherlands, Belgium, and later Germany and the United States because their imports of raw materials and exports of finished goods required trading partners who were not their equals in terms of technological, social and infrastructural development.

Even though the 'global' dimensions on which trade takes place have remained the same.[27] Today, most trade takes place between the most developed parts of the world: North America, the European Union, and individual countries in the Far East, led by Japan (see Table 5.3). Seriously underdeveloped countries are of only marginal commercial interest to these major trading partners.

Since the beginning of the 1980s, international investment patterns have shown a marked rise, foreign investment has grown in most directions, and together with the increase in size and weight of multinational firms (not in themselves an invention of the twentieth century), this has complicated any analysis of what 'national' interests in trade might constitute.

The emerging pattern shows that whereas most trade takes place between the extremely developed areas, there is fierce competition between

Table 5.3: The leading trading nations of the world
(a) Imports in US$ billion

	1993	1994
USA	603.4	689.2
Germany	329.7	370.1
Japan	241.7	266.5
Great Britain	206.3	220.0
France	200.8	217.9
Italy	146.7	160.4
Canada	139.1	148.7
Hong Kong	138.7	148.3
The Netherlands	121.6	121.4
Belgium-Luxembourg	119.5	120.2
China	103.9	115.7
Singapore	85.2	99.6
South Korea	83.8	97.6
Spain	81.9	87.5
Taiwan	77.0	82.4
Mexico	50.1	79.4
Switzerland	56.7	61.7

(b) Exports in US$ billion

	1993	1994
USA	464.8	512.7
Germany	365.4	414.5
Japan	362.4	387.9
France	206.3	220.7
Great Britain	181.6	196.0
Italy	164.5	178.7
Canada	145.2	159.0
Hong Kong	135.2	136.5
Netherlands	131.2	127.2
Belgium-Luxembourg	123.2	124.4
China	91.7	121.0
Taiwan	83.0	93.5
Singapore	74.0	93.0
South Korea	82.2	89.8
Spain	62.9	69.1
Switzerland	58.7	63.0
Mexico	30.2	60.8

Source: Mario v. Baratta (ed.), *Der Fischer Weltalmanach '96* (Frankfurt/Main: Fischer Taschenbuch Verlag, 1995), p. 1083.

their industries and companies for export markets. Trade is thus accompanied by substantial friction and individual disagreements which trouble relations between the governments of the trading countries. Though many of the governments of the highly developed countries believe that free trade is generally in the best interest of their own (modern, efficient and therefore competitive) industries, there are production areas in each country (and not only in the developing countries) which they see as needing protection in the form of tariffs on imports from rival industries abroad. Import taxes imposed by one country are invariably disliked by the industries of other countries whose export products are thus deprived of their competitive edge.

Would a TAFTA arrangement further the North Atlantic countries' common interest *vis-à-vis* their competitors in the Far East, and move competition from the Atlantic to the Pacific? Or better still, could the world economy be managed through a system which benefits all sides and contains what would otherwise be ever sharper competition between the leading trading nations? A purely North Atlantic solution could not possibly be regarded as totally satisfactory. It would necessarily be seen as an extremely objectionable, indeed hostile, policy by the dynamic Far Eastern countries. The second solution would be ideal, if only it proved to be a realistic possibility. Much depends on whether such a mutually advantageous solution could be invented (and it is clear that it would never be advantageous to all aspects of every national economy of every participating country). But much also depends on the overall performance of the world economy, and on the efficient use of limited resources. It is useful here to cast a brief look at the prehistory of the World Trade Organization.

From Bretton Woods and GATT to WTO
In the immediate post-Second World War period, the United States led an initiative which aimed at managing these differences through the establishment of the 'Bretton Woods' institutions, including the World Bank and the International Monetary Fund. At the same time, it initiated the first General Agreement on Tariffs and Trade, concluded in 1947, designed to reduce tariffs between countries to all sides' overall benefit. It was originally intended to be accompanied by an international trade organization, a specialized agency of the United Nations, to help settle disputes over the application of trade rules as established by GATT. The Geneva GATT Round of 1947 was followed by the Annecy Round (1949), the Torquay Round (1951), and another round in Geneva (1956). A further round of negotiations in Geneva followed: the Dillon Round of 1960–61.

As the number of contracting parties grew, subsequent negotiations took ever longer to reach agreement: between 1961 and 1986, the number of countries which contracted into GATT rose from 26 to 108. The Kennedy Round began in 1964 and went on until 1967. The Tokyo Round lasted from 1973 to 1979. Finally, the Uruguay Round, begun in 1986, was only concluded in 1994. All sides then felt it necessary to modify the system of negotiations by introducing new arbitration procedures under the aegis of a World Trade Organization, which became operational on 1 January 1995.

The WTO has 128 contracting parties, and a further 30 states have expressed the desire to join (which means accepting the agreements enshrined in the Uruguay Round's final act and all previous rounds). The act included agreement on the following points:

- tariffs imposed by the industrialized countries were reduced by over a third, while developing countries agreed to freeze theirs at a maximum of 35–40%;
- intellectual property rights were to be afforded better protection;
- anti-dumping rules were to be improved, subventions limited, and henceforth the WTO is to act as independent arbiter on disputes pertaining to these areas;
- non-tariff barriers to the import of agrarian products were to be transformed into tariffs, themselves to be reduced progressively by the industrialized countries. Export subsidies were to be reduced by over a third, as was the quantity of subsidized exports.

Agreement on agricultural issues was not complete. There remain many points of friction here arising from the protectionist attitude of both the US and certain European governments (concerning particularly beef and dairy products, excluded from the final GATT agreement of 1994). There was no agreement on audiovisual trade (where protectionist measures are defended by France), on financial services and on shipping services (a particular area of US protectionism). The civil aviation industry, and areas of government-financed public procurement, were also excluded from GATT 94. In preparation for the first WTO ministerial meeting, scheduled to take place in Singapore in December 1996, negotiations are under way among the members states concerning the issues of liberalization of the markets for telecommunications and maritime transport (a protected sector of the US economy).

The aims and tasks of the WTO are to work towards worldwide free trade in order to ensure the most efficient use of economic resources, to effect an increase in living standards, employment figures and real income worldwide. The WTO is governed by the following principles:

- reciprocity: concessions made between members must be of equal benefit to both parties;
- liberalization: the aim of the WTO is to continue further with the multilateral reduction of tariffs and non-tariff barriers to trade;
- non-discrimination: any tariff and trade advantages negotiated between any two members of the WTO are to apply also to all other members. Developing countries continue to be exempted in part from this rule. But the GATT of 1947 in its Article XXIV also conceded the possibility of free trade areas and customs unions: this was limited in the GATT 94, making it more difficult to exclude other GATT members from most-favoured-nation status.

With the creation of the WTO at the end of GATT 94, the contracting parties forced one another to accept the WTO's rules by joining it, or else to face exclusion from most-favoured-nation status in trade with WTO members. Membership also binds signatories to follow more predictable and constant national economic policies. The WTO guarantees that neither the EU nor the United States can turn itself into a tariff-protected fortress *vis-à-vis* other contracting parties.

Yet the WTO can only work incrementally towards the abolition of tariffs and non-tariff barriers which are still obstructing increased exports from the EU, the US or indeed Canada to Far Eastern industrialized countries. The WTO will certainly be a useful forum for addressing many of the issues that arise over the differing interests of member states. It is only a stepping stone towards further tariff reductions and the abolition of protectionist measures, not yet a crucial institution opening up a free trade area among all its members. Friction and competition may continue.

Problems beyond the reach of the WTO
Trade frictions and policies are of course also discussed in other multilateral fora, such as the summits of the G7 (the seven most important economic powers: Britain, Canada, France, Germany, Italy, Japan, the United States). They are also negotiated in the Organization for Economic Cooperation and Development (OECD), created in 1960 to plan,

coordinate and deepen economic cooperation and development of its member states, and to coordinate the administration of aid to developing countries. Apart from the 16 states which joined its institutional predecessor as recipients of Marshall Aid,* the OECD counts among its members the Federal Republic of Germany (since its inception in 1949), Spain (since 1959), Canada and the United States (since 1960), Japan (since 1964), Finland (since 1969), Australia (since 1971), New Zealand (since 1973) and finally Mexico (since 1994). South Korea, the Czech Republic, Hungary, Poland and Slovakia have stated their interest in joining.

Nevertheless, the competences of the OECD are limited. The main actors (in terms of legislating and imposing tariffs, rules and regulations) continue to be national governments or, in the case of the European Union, the Commission. Further, friction remains a problem even within these fora. Examples abound where individual member states or groups within the OECD or GATT/WTO do not back one another in negotiations with third parties, and yet reap the benefits (and particularly the concessions made by both sides) of bilateral agreements subsequently concluded. In short, within these fora, EU members are just as much rivals of the NAFTA states, particularly the United States, as they are rivals of Japan. Such rivalries loom large in a landscape not dominated by defence since the end of the Cold War.

This means that, on the one hand, important contributions have been made by the use of arbitration on behalf of the general interest, rejecting settlements which benefit one side more than another. Yet on the other hand, competition and clashes of economic interest have become more pronounced in recent years. All sides fear that, as in previous centuries, economic competition might turn into hostility, instability and even insecurity. Though it is fortunately difficult to imagine military clashes between North Americans and west and central Europeans, profound insecurity would nevertheless result if the need for harmonization of strategic security policies were overshadowed by more acute perceptions of economic rivalry.

The general economic situation thus becomes crucial. If the world economy were in the prosperous, thriving state of the 1960s, competition for markets would not be quite so keen. Now, however, there is a clear sense that the North Americans and the EU are wooing the same potential markets in the Far East and Southeast Asia. There is harsh competition

*Belgium, Denmark, France, Greece, Britain, Ireland, Iceland, Italy, Luxembourg, the Netherlands, Norway, Austria, Portugal, Sweden, Switzerland and Turkey all first joined the OECD's predecessor, the OEEC, in 1948.

for lucrative orders of military equipment, as we shall see in Chapter 6.

Economic aid issues are, in part, what both the OECD and WTO were designed to address. The WTO, particularly, could help to shape the economic and legal structures of developing countries while they are modernizing (or, in the case of the central and eastern Europeans, liberalizing) their economies. The problem remains that these countries are finding it extremely difficult to cross the threshold from being economic liabilities to their trading partners to being partners worth making concessions to. With their present underdeveloped social, legal and economic structures, they are stuck in a vicious circle of inadequate legal protection for investment, inadequate infrastructures, and an inadequately educated workforce, leading to inadequate returns on investments and hence lack of interest among investors. Nothing can guarantee the crucial impetus needed to end this vicious circle.

All this spells danger of increased tension between the industrialized nations and the underdeveloped countries, particularly those in Africa and some parts of Asia which have little hope of improvement. Insecurity and war, sustained by poverty and competition for vital resources, could be the fate of these poorest areas of the world; the industrialized nations will have little incentive to become involved.

A key question running through this economic level of European–North American relations is whether their aims are primarily regional or primarily global. The global destiny was suggested by Douglas Hurd, then British Foreign Secretary, when he spoke of a 'pathfinder role' for Europe and North America in international trade, working together 'to persuade others to join us to make the system more effective'.[28] His successor, Malcolm Rifkind, shares his optimism about the beneficial effects of such cooperation beyond the North Atlantic area, and casts his country in the role of champion of free trade in Europe.[29] Though it is stressed on all sides that nobody wants to see one as an alternative to the other,[30] the danger remains that one might detract from the effort spent on the other.

But little planning is devoted in either context to what is probably thought of as an excessively altruistic consideration: how to bring the developing countries into the developed world, the prosperity of which WTO is (and a TAFTA would be) designed to enhance.

Chapter 6

Atlanticism vs. European integration?

> Europe must have her own personality in her own defence ...
> Certainly, ... it is necessary that she should also have allies, that is
> to say that she should unite her defence to that of other countries
> which also want to defend themselves against the same adversary,
> but which, in order to do so, have their own direction, their plan,
> and their own means. In other words, the Americans... . [Then]
> there is NATO. What is NATO? That is the sum of the Americans,
> the Europeans and some others. But that is not the defence of
> Europe by Europe, it is the defence of Europe by the Americans.
> We need another NATO. First of all, Europe needs her own de-
> fence. That Europe must be allied to America.[1]

A great deal of what has been described about recent developments in
transatlantic relations remains unintelligible if it is not acknowledged
that a sense of rivalry has characterized some aspects of European–
American relations. The rivalry is all the stranger in view of the overall
and long-standing support that the United States has given to European
integration since the immediate postwar years, even if there were elements of ambiguity in Washington's treatment of the Europeans.

The United States and European integration

American postwar policy towards Europe was driven not only by anti-
communism, but also by the desire to make a lasting peace among the
Europeans themselves. Marshall Aid was given to the Europeans on
condition that they worked together through the OEEC, later replaced by
the OECD. European integration, first in the form of the Brussels Treaty

of 1948 (which formed the Western Union, later renamed Western European Union), followed by the European Coal and Steel Community (ECSC) of 1950, and the (abortive) project for a European Defence Community (1950–54), was strongly supported by the US, which even threatened an 'agonizing reappraisal' if the Europeans did not show sincere commitment to integration and cooperation among themselves. European integration was thus encouraged, indeed in part driven, by the US desire to end the long history of fratricidal wars among the Europeans, which by the twentieth century had developed the tendency to suck in the United States.

Moreover, US governments have wanted the Europeans to put their own house in order and pay for their own defence. From the earliest post-Cold War period, US governments have wanted to see Europe prosperous and able to defend itself, but not dependent upon US aid. Marshall Aid was intended to enable the Europeans to look after themselves, rather than to be a perpetual burden on the United States, as they were to become despite the positive effects of this aid. Indeed, it was President Kennedy who first spoke about the two pillars of NATO, one American and one European, which were needed to keep the edifice from falling down.[2]

Since then, Washington has on the whole remained supportive of European integration, to an extent that makes nonsense of any theory of US imperialism trying to colonize Europe.[3] Occasionally, however, it became jealous when excluded from agreements in Europe, whether or not these had a recognizably anti-American flavour. Certainly, exclusively European cooperation furthered the peace-ensuring habit of working together without US supervision, and the United States has welcomed this on one level. But on another level, American policy-makers fear that the Europeans may present them with a list of demands, expecting them to foot the bill without having had a chance to specify conditions. This has periodically resulted in US countermeasures of the divide and rule sort. More than once, Washington has attempted to claw back the initiative on issues it had originally recognized as purely European. In sum, the US attitude towards European integration has at times been ambivalent, contributing to the uncertainty that bedevilled both European integration and the restructuring of NATO after the end of the Cold War.

To be fair, however, the Europeans have but themselves to blame if they allow themselves to be divided and ruled, and if, after 45 years of European integration, they are still unable to produce a sole interlocutor for a US president. Representing Europe today in matters of foreign and security policy are the President of the European Commission, Jacques Santer; the leader of the country that happens to be presiding over the

European Council (comprising the heads of government of the EU member states); the Commissioner dealing with foreign affairs; and any leader of a European state who happens to be visiting Washington as self-appointed spokesman for Europe. One proposal put forward by President Chirac of France has been to add another figure to this list, a 'Monsieur PESC' (Mr/Ms Common Foreign and Security Policy, CFSP). But this proposal does little to change the fact that there is no sole, streamlined, clearly defined centre of power in Europe, that the state governments are determinedly clinging to their sovereignty and are prepared to go behind the back of the European Commission they themselves created. The Canadian government experienced this in the dispute about cod fishing with Spain in mid-1995: while the European Union initially showed a common front, this soon crumbled, and one state government after another broke ranks, siding with Canada or at any rate no longer with their EU partner Spain in the dispute. Whenever outside pressure is skilfully applied, European unity crumbles easily under the conflicting short-term interests of different states. The resulting divisions and chaos can hardly be blamed on the outsider, which then only has the option of trying to draw the greatest advantage for its own state from the situation.

From both the European and any other state's point of view, it is thus clearly a complication that there are so many bilateral and ill-coordinated channels of European–American relations, with maximum scope for misunderstandings and confusion. A key question on any transatlantic agenda is thus which institutional framework – NATO? the EU–US dialogue? with or without Canada? – should be the main channel of communication. If European integration does not progress, particularly in the foreign and security policy fields, transatlantic relations will be no more than the sum of respective bilateral relations in these fields. It should therefore continue to be in the interest of the United States for the EU to transform itself into an independent, often phlegmatic, but on most major issues dependable partner. Otherwise it will remain, as at present, a harem of feminists, each wanting exclusivity in relations with the United States, each fiercely jealous of rivals, and yet each asserting her sovereignty and independence with great conviction.

The rationale of European integration and the French paradigm

Understanding of US attitudes towards European integration can only be furthered by acknowledging that there is at times an anti-American twist to European policies. First of all, it must be noted that the rationale underlying European integration only partially overlaps with that underlying transatlantic cooperation. While post-Second World War European integration is also built on common values, there is a need for closeness and for a degree of integration which simply do not apply on a transatlantic scale. Closeness is needed because a thousand years of intra-European enmity must be overcome, because deep-rooted distrust exists, which can only be uprooted by ever greater familiarity and transparency, ever closer cooperation and interdependence. The spectres of the past that reasserted themselves when Germany was reunited – from fears of a German–Russian understanding and betrayal of the West *à la* Rapallo, to nightmares of a 'Fourth Reich' dominating Europe – are proof that more trust, more mutual understanding, more integration are needed in Europe. This is also in the interest of the United States and Canada, and should be fully supported by them.

There is another rationale underlying European integration, however, and it is found most often, but not only, in France. It is recognition of the weakness of the individual European powers, if taken by themselves, and nostalgia for their status in the nineteenth and even early twentieth centuries. It is the conviction that they can only play a leading role on a world scale if they unite the strength of other European states with their own. So far, this is again in the interest of both the United States and Canada, as they are looking for 'like-minded' powers to help them protect and project their values throughout the world.

But the history of Franco-US relations since 1945, when the US consciously began to play the role of world policeman, has been one of rivalry, as noted in Chapter 2. France is imbued with the same missionary zeal, and the same self-perception as a beacon of progress for the rest of the world, as the United States. France's *mission civilisatrice* is in competition with the propagation abroad of the 'American way of life'. France smarted under US tutelage in NATO from 1954 until its disengagement from NATO's military integration in 1966. And France's commitment to independence and sovereignty, as opposed to its subordination to the US in the alliance, has become one of the founding myths of the Fifth Republic.

But this Fifth Republic has come to recognize the limits of what it can do as a lone sovereign nation-state. The Gulf war was among the most important learning exercises in this context. Even under President Mitterrand, the sanctity of French sovereignty began to be seen as negotiable, in return for European integration inspired by French ideas.

Atlanticism vs. European integration?

And the new, post-de Gaullian French *certaine idée de l'Europe* makes Europe America's equal on a world stage on all levels – economic, political and military. And this equality could only be assured if Europe did not remain totally dependent on the United States for its defence. While no French president since de Gaulle has ever wanted to tear up the North Atlantic Treaty or give up the safety-net of the US commitment to European security in Article 5, there has been a clear wish to reduce European reliance on the United States in more limited contingencies. Again, there is much ground here for convergence of interests between the two countries.

But both the French and the Americans have visceral objections to fighting under the command of foreign nationals, and this has bedevilled their relationship since the haggling over command post assignments during NATO's infancy in the early 1950s. It was still a key problem during the Gulf war, where French forces only fought under the 'operational' command of the American coalition force leadership (meaning that every order could be vetoed by the French government), and continues to be one today: the application of the CJTF proposals has been complicated by this since their inception. There is thus a real sense of rivalry, which tends to revolve around command structures and assignments of forces. That this issue is one which is kept alive by both sides is symbolized in US opposition since the beginning of the alliance to any suggestion that the Supreme Allied Commander Europe (SACEUR) should be a European.* It was also symbolized by the suspicion with which US (and also British) leaders greeted the Franco-German creation of the Eurocorps and the concept of a European defence identity.

The rise and fall of a European defence identity
To consider the long-standing dispute about the distribution of power within NATO, we must turn briefly to its origins. Before NATO, there was the Western Union (WU), created by the Brussels Pact of 1948, and designed on the one hand to help the West Europeans protect each other against a potentially resurgent Germany, and on the other to help them fend off the Soviet threat (which was still taking the form of communist putsches, rather than military invasions). It was a signal of solidarity which later gave the North Americans confidence that their engagement in Europe would not be built on sand; it thus made NATO possible. In 1950, the WU allowed its defence planning organization to be absorbed

*The chief military command post in NATO in Europe had always been occupied by an American.

94

into the North Atlantic Treaty Organization. In 1954 the WU, now the WEU, admitted West Germany and Italy.

In the 1980s, there was a move to revive the WEU. Europeans who saw Washington, first, as unduly risk-prone in its relations with Moscow, and, after 1985, as unduly compromise-prone, sought to build up the WEU as a European fall-back organization, to hedge against US unilateralism. The end of the Cold War, as we have seen, confirmed an integrationist tendency in Europe, and, particularly in France, the wish to emancipate the continent from American predominance. This revived interest in the WEU.

The first years after the end of the Cold War were riddled with transatlantic tensions about the effects of closer European cooperation on transatlantic relations. The French and the Germans, joined later by the Italians, proposed at the end of 1990 that the WEU should be integrated directly into the EU, to become its defence arm.[4] This proposal was quashed by British and Dutch, but also US, opposition.[5] On the eve of the WEU summit early in 1991, a US Under-Secretary of State, Reginald Bartholomew, addressed a letter to the European WEU members warning them not to take steps which might undermine NATO.[6] The flutter he caused had barely subsided when Secretary of State James Baker repeated the message, loud and clear.[7] European integrationists angrily replied that the United States did not have a veto power over European defence integration.[8] The North Atlantic Council (NAC)* at its Copenhagen meeting in June 1991 had secured for the twelve EEC members the right to adopt their own, collective security policy.[9]

Nevertheless the Americans remained unhappy about the situation. Another issue causing them heartache was the Eurocorps. The Eurocorps' origins go back to President François Mitterrand's and Chancellor Helmut Kohl's decision announced on 13 November 1987 to form a brigade of 4,200 mainly young conscript soldiers from both countries. The principal object was to further the trust between French and Germans.[10] The brigade became operational in October 1990 in Böblingen, in the Federal Republic of Germany, just in time for the German reunification which was causing the French so much discomfort.

Although its military value was little more than symbolic, it represented a departure from the Gaullist orthodoxy that French forces must not be put under a foreign commander, so was a step of major political importance. When on 1 October 1991 General Helmut Neubauer took

*The supreme political authority in NATO, comprising the heads of government or state of the NATO member states.

over the command of this unit from his French predecessor, it was the first time since 1966 that this iron rule had been broken.[11]

The step from Franco-German brigade to Eurocorps again had a mainly European symbolism. France's initial reactions to Germany's reunification had not been those that Bonn might have expected from its 'special' friends across the Rhine. The formation of the Eurocorps was intended to make up for this, and provide a figleaf for the continued presence of French forces in Germany.[12] On 14 October 1991, Chancellor Kohl and President Mitterrand presented a draft for the Maastricht Treaty, proposing that the WEU should become the defence arm of the EU, but that for the time being no EU member should be allowed to accede to the WEU unless it was already a member of NATO. In this way, it was made clear that the Franco-German proposal should aim not at moving the WEU outside the NATO framework, but at strengthening the WEU as the European pillar of NATO. Then, as a postcript, the proposal added:

> Franco-German military cooperation will be strengthened beyond the existing brigade. The strengthened Franco-German units could thus become the nucleus of a European corps capable of including the forces of other member-states of the WEU. This new structure could equally become the model of a closer military cooperation among the member-states of the WEU.[13]

The German government later affirmed that this European corps, with its headquarters in Strasbourg, pointed to the significance of France's readiness to accept this concept of military integration with its European allies. It also heralded the first instance of the cross-stationing of German military on French soil, in itself a sign that France now accepted Germany as an equal partner. Nor would the European corps be outside NATO structures.[14] The German government affirmed repeatedly that the German forces assigned to this corps would not be withdrawn from NATO.[15] To understand the German position another factor has to be taken into account. As we have seen, Germany needed to adapt to the idea that it might be called upon to send forces abroad. Seen from the other side, in view of the fears Germany's neighbours near and far have in its respect, German military actions alongside allies might be more acceptable if cloaked in 'Euro'-multilateralism.

Nevertheless, concerns that the Eurocorps might weaken NATO persisted, particularly in the United States, but also in Britain, the Netherlands and Italy.[16] But the Spanish government under Felipe González showed considerable interest in the project, conditional upon the Corps wearing a NATO hat and a WEU hat.[17] Belgium also joined the Corps.[18] Four years later, on 1 October 1995, the Eurocorps was to become operational with 35,000 soldiers assigned to it.[19]

But the US government showed little sang-froid with regard to the matter. Several heavy-handed *démarches* were made in European capitals, reflecting the fear that the Europeans were planning things behind American backs.[20] At the opening of the Rome summit of NATO in November 1991, President Bush stated:

> our premise is that the American role in the defence and affairs of Europe will not be made superfluous by European union. If our premise is wrong – if, my friends, your ultimate aim is to provide independently for your own defence, the time to tell us is today.[21]

Put in these stark terms, and coming but three months after the sobering August putsch in Moscow, the Europeans unsurprisingly had nothing but reassurance to offer to the US President. This was reflected in the Treaty on European Union (TEU) initialled in Maastricht the following month, which stopped short of integrating the purely European WEU into the European Union, emphasizing instead the continuing importance of NATO for Europe's security.[22] Nevertheless, the attitude of the US was vexing for those of its allies who felt that they had been acting in good faith, merely trying to do as it had urged them to for decades.[23]

While the TEU did not stipulate the integration of the WEU into the EU, it left this option open. Obviously, the incomplete overlap of membership was a tangible obstacle to an immediate fusion of the two organizations, but the position of the British government was just as much of an impediment. Consistently, London and Washington (joined more often than not by Bonn) sought to secure a 'right of first refusal' for NATO, so that an issue should only pass to the WEU for handling if NATO (that is, the United States and Canada) had refused to be associated.[24]

The question marks about US willingness to become involved in minor contingencies in Europe led France to continue to explore two options: either the enhancement of the capability of the WEU to take action (particularly if the United States showed no interest in becoming involved), or the restructuring of NATO itself, giving its European pillar more weight. The last Socialist French Defence Minister, Pierre Joxe, wanted to enable France to assert its views within the alliance, rather than from outside, against it. Even in autumn 1992, he advocated a rapprochement with the planning committees of NATO.[25] This was quoted enthusiastically by both Secretary General Manfred Wörner and the Atlanticists within France (who since 1966 had been the weaker political force).[26] But Gaullist orthodoxy still rejected the reintegration of French forces into any permanent NATO military command structure. The stronger view in France insisted that French forces could operate in the Balkan war in a loose, intergovernmental WEU framework, but not within an integrated NATO structure.

The CJTF compromise, and continuing French insistence on the differences between European and US policies in Bosnia, were interpreted in some places as a French plot to undermine NATO and replace it, step by step, by a purely European defence alliance.[27] It seemed in 1994 that times were favouring the strengthening of a European defence identity, that is the WEU, or a WEU linked to the EU's Common Foreign and Security Policy, which (according to the Maastricht Treaty) might in time lead to a common European defence. Europe, it seemed, was well advised to take charge of its own business.[28]

But instead, four developments at once turned the tide. The British government dug in their heels; the Atlanticist forces in Germany, led by both the Minister of Defence and the Minister of Foreign Affairs, declared NATO irreplaceable; the Clinton administration finally decided to assume full-scale leadership to pacify Bosnia and maintain peace; and in France, successive governments opted for a gradual rapprochement with the NATO headquarters fora in Brussels.

The final development was a long time in the making. De Gaulle's own decision to withdraw from the integrated military structure of NATO was not his preferred option: he would have liked NATO to be restructured to give more weight and autonomy to its European members within the Alliance, and to put France in a leading role, in a three-power directorate together with the US and Britain. Thus even within the Gaullist RPR, there were politicians and advisers who sought to realize de Gaulle's preferred option through a rapprochement with NATO.

The number of those advising such a course of action had risen since the end of the Cold War. A small but important concession was made when the French government in winter 1992/3 agreed that French forces assigned to the Eurocorps could, upon the decision of the French president in time of war, fight within the integrated military structure of NATO.[29] An agreement was signed in January 1993 between SACEUR General Shalikashvili with the Inspector-General of the Bundeswehr, General Naumann, and the Chief of the French Joint General Staff,

Admiral Joxe. On its terms, the Eurocorps can fight under SACEUR, should the leaders of France and Germany decide this in given circumstances.[30] Shortly before assuming office as Minister of Foreign Affairs in March 1993, Alain Juppé had noted his interest in participating 'in a certain number of organs of the Alliance, such as the Defence Planning Committee', while firmly dismissing the option of total reintegration into the military structures of NATO.[31] Similar views were stated by his colleague in the rue St Dominique, François Léotard.[32] From May 1993, France was represented by a general in the Military Committee of NATO when joint military action in former Yugoslavia was discussed.[33] In October 1993, Léotard let it be known that the return of the French Defence Minister (himself) and the Chief of the French General Staff at NATO meetings would be addressed in the new Defence White Book.[34] This was indeed the case, and the logic was spelt out: it was based on the assumption that the Americans 'might hold back when it comes to addressing questions which concern the security and stability of the [European] continent, but which do not affect [American] strategic interests directly'. NATO would therefore have to change (also in view of the new missions it would take on), and France wanted to be present at the restructuring.[35] In September 1994, France was for the first time since 1966 represented by its defence minister at a meeting of NATO defence ministers, but only for the item on the agenda which concerned joint action in Bosnia.[36] Nevertheless, Léotard still seemed to be banking on the possibility that a European defence identity could be promoted independently if complementarily.[37]

One year later, the new government under Alain Juppé as Prime Minister, appointed by the new President Jacques Chirac, decided on the full re-entry of France into NATO's Military Committee, no longer limited to issues of out-of-area action.[38] Abandoning France's previous commitment to promoting the WEU, Jacques Chirac has now chosen the path of working for a reformed NATO, in which the European pillar will become stronger: 'A strong Alliance necessitates a strong Europe, capable of assuming a greater part of the common burden.'[39]

The background to this was in part the determination of the British government not to allow the WEU to be fused with the EU at the 1996 Intergovernmental Conference, if at all: at the WEU ministers' meeting in Madrid in November 1995, Britain, in a minority of one, persuaded its partners to include the option of preserving the separation between the EU and WEU in their policy statement.[40] Other countries were not very keen on an immediate fusion, although none but Britain wanted to put the 'never' option on the agenda. Neither the integral part of the development of the EU still postulated by the Maastricht Treaty, nor the European pillar of NATO, the WEU today has a less certain future than it did at the time the Maastricht Treaty was negotiated.

This raises the question as to what future there is for an *independent* European defence identity. The Eurocorps exists, and it has been suggested that it might serve as the hard core of a European rapid reaction force under WEU auspices.[41] But the WEU had essentially only been kept alive by France's determination not to be represented in the planning organs of NATO, and thus to necessitate the existence of another forum for European agreement with France. No doubt the WEU will continue to serve other useful functions such as the association of the former neutral and central-east European countries with west European military planning.[42]

But as the key defence planning body for the EU, let alone as the prime defence organization for Europe, the WEU has once again become a sleeping beauty (Josef Joffe). Any European defence identity and any EU common foreign, security and defence policy formulated by a qualified majority vote, independently of NATO or the transatlantic link, are nothing but dreams lingering in the enchanted forest. As the WEU Secretary General José Cutileiro commented prophetically, 'As far as I know, [the WEU] will not be doing anything else in the foreseeable future'.[43]

US or European leadership in NATO?

The difficulties in US–European defence relations were a function first of the Bush administration's determination to retain the leadership of the Atlantic Alliance, and then of the Clinton administration's preoccupation with non-military matters, which left a leadership vacuum in the alliance.

With the disappearance of the uniting threat, those who saw the alliance mainly as a temporary coincidence of national self-interests speculated from 1989 onwards that NATO would henceforth play a much reduced role, if it continued to play one at all. It was 'thought that NATO could be put in a glass case, placed on a shelf with a label on it: "break glass in case of revived Russian threat".'[44] This view was championed above all by the French,[45] but there were those on the other side of the Atlantic who believed it was no longer useful for Canada and the US to remain committed to NATO.[46] Repeatedly during the 1989–95 period, even staunch NATO supporters despaired of the Alliance's chances of survival. The notion that it was withering away was encouraged by the simultaneous drive towards European integration in which there were traces of a quest for emancipation from US tutelage. Further European integration was supported by Spain and Greece in part for that reason, while the Germans, Belgians, Italians and Dutch were more concerned to prevent a renationalization of European defence policies after the end of the Cold War and German reunification.

Some, however, clinging to the common values of the North Atlantic nations, were determined not to give up the *acquis* of the Atlantic alliance. There were several motivations for this: the continuing wish for US rather than European leadership was certainly to be found in Denmark and the Benelux countries. Italy and Britain feared for their bilateral special relationships with the US. And several countries, among them Britain and (after some initial naïveté) Germany, felt that the Russian military (conventional and nuclear) potential could still only be offset by America. American leaders noted that their bases in Europe had been very useful in the Gulf war, and that their influence in European politics would be reduced very substantially if they gave up their military trump. Much to France's surprise, the majority view within the alliance was thus that NATO was worth preserving, indeed, that it should be reformed to enable it to take on new tasks.

Yet precisely as consensus upon this point began to emerge in Europe, US leadership was lacking. The restructuring of NATO's forces, the drastic reduction of the North American troop strengths in Europe, and the long period of US reluctance to send ground forces to the former Yugoslavia raised question marks as to the future of the US commitment to Europe. After decades in which the expression 'vital interest' had been very loosely interpreted (to mean 'very important'), and had been used to open up defence spending, the Clinton administration opted for a more limited (and more literal) use of the term (as an issue affecting the very survival of the US).[47] Even in justifying US leadership in Bosnia since the end of 1995, Clinton has not used the term 'vital', but described 'strategic interests' as being at stake.[48] This change of emphasis, coupled with the force build-down in Europe, led Europeans to suspect that 'President Clinton's new foreign policy is one of creeping disengagement'.[49]

A turning point was reached in May 1993, when a senior US State Department official, Peter Tarnoff, told journalists that US economic interests were paramount: in view of the limited resources it commands, the US must 'define the extent of its commitment and make a commitment commensurate with those realities. This may on occasion fall short of what some Americans would like and others would hope for'.[50] This was then vehemently denied by other officials who urged Europeans not to pay any heed to the opinions expressed by official 'Brand X'.[51] Ever since, there has been a stream of denials that the US has relinquished its leading role in Europe.[52] The need for US leadership became the leitmotif of the US defence statement of 1995, albeit tempered with the words that 'our involvement must be carefully tailored to serve our interests and priorities [and] … will be more circumscribed when other regional or multilateral actors are better positioned to act than we are.'[53]

Despite the assertion in the statement that 'American leadership in the world has never been more important', European doubts as to the US commitment were not allayed until the end of 1995. At regular intervals, the US commitment to Europe was put in doubt, just as it had been in 1957 when Sputnik ended US invulnerability, and well-placed defence commentators saw the need for the Europeans to assume the lead within the new NATO.[54] But an important consideration was the determined insistence on the need for US leadership and presence in Europe by the central and east European countries. Whatever advantages were offered by their association with the WEU, they did not cease to remind the West that it was NATO they wished to join, under American leadership, to balance whatever was to the east of them. Moreover, despite their supposed neutral heritage, Finland and Sweden look to NATO and America to protect them, a task they would not entrust to the WEU.[55]

The leadership crisis, and particularly the long stalemate in Bosnia, thus led to a debate about the future internal functioning of the Alliance, and the respective roles of Europe and the United States within it. Having accepted that NATO will be the main framework for any defensive action, the new French government is trying to set the pace and direction of its future development. Jacques Chirac and Alain Juppé have noted that they intend to work for a grand reform and restructuring of NATO.[56] An independent European defence identity will not now come into existence, but the French vision of Europe still dictates some greater degree of equality among Europe and America, even if it is within NATO. The two-pillar structure called for by President Kennedy more than three decades ago is now the model for further development. President Chirac's agenda, as explained by his Defence Minister Charles Millon, is NATO reform, and the items on the agenda would have found de Gaulle's thorough approval: the confirmation of a true European defence identity, a reform of the structure of NATO and a security pact between NATO and Russia to reassure Moscow about the effects of NATO widening. Millon said France wanted to see the emergence of a real European general staff within NATO which is not just duplication, a general staff that is in direct contact with its forces, because the future is one of variable geometry operations, based on one pillar or the other, with a number of different participants as appropriate for each [particular] case.[57]

As one commentator put it mischievously: 'the "battle" over European defence is not over: it has merely changed its battlefield'.[58]

Trade or competition?
Another area where this battle is being waged is trade. Among EU members the Chirac-Juppé French government is the least enthusiastic about the TAFTA project. And France has long asserted that a defence-industrial battle is being waged between Europe and America, the outcome of which will determine how far Europe can ever hope to be independent of the United States.[59]

The most crucial areas in this context are satellite intelligence, airlift capability and other major systems procurement.[60] Another constituent myth of the Fifth Republic is that dependence on another nation for defence procurement is in itself a surrender of sovereignty and independence.[61]

With regard to airlift capability and indeed aircraft production more generally, the French are not the only ones in Europe who argue that European industries have a considerable interest in the continued existence of European aircraft production. As unit costs are inversely proportional to numbers of units built, all aircraft industries (and indeed the governments buying the aircraft) have a strong interest in large production runs. At the same time, the market for exports of state-of-the-art fighter aircraft is conditioned by the unreliability of potential buyers as partners in international relations, as the French learned to their cost in the Gulf war, when Iraq used the same French-built fighter-planes as the French.

Perhaps even more crucial is the issue of satellite intelligence. The French were shocked by their degree of blindness in the Gulf war and reliance on the titbits which the United States was willing to share with them (the special intelligence-sharing relationship between the United States and United Kingdom had of course long been a thorn in their flesh).[62] It was again the last Socialist Defence Minister, Pierre Joxe, who supported plans for a European satellite system to give Europe independent access to intelligence.[63] The WEU has since opened its own satellite information analysis centre in Torrejon in Spain, fed by imagery from the French-Italian-Spanish Helios 1-A satellite that was launched in July

103

1995, and further satellites are planned.[64] An interesting causality is at work here: the inability of an individual state (France) to bear the cost of this project has forced it into sharing the expenses but thus also the images derived from satellites with other states which agreed to help finance it.[65] But with intelligence integration of this sort, the ground is prepared for more political and defence cooperation, on the basis of shared information and analysis.

The United States, however, was not impartial to this development. Indeed, it is often accused by the French of wanting to establish a hegemony in major sectors of the defence industry.[66] The sense of rivalry between the United States and European integration can be seen in US attempts to forestall German cooperation with France on further satellite projects, even though business interest alone may have been the major factor in US policy-making. A watershed was reached at the end of 1995, when it became known that the United States had proposed a deal to Germany which would have permitted it to buy into the US Keyhole satellite programme at a lower cost. This, in the view of the French defence correspondent Jacques Isnard, would have given the FRG a status 'practically equivalent' to that of the United Kingdom in intelligence-sharing with the United States. After a lengthy delay, Kohl declined this offer and on 7 December 1995 signed the agreement on the construction of Helios 2 and Horus with Chirac.[67]

Again, the French view postulates that Europe, in order to be the equal of the United States, must be independent of it in its defence procurement and intelligence. This was the lesson the French drew from the Suez crisis of 1956. Since their own acrimonious revision of defence policy, begun after the Suez crisis, the British, by contrast, have seen no alternative to 'interdependence' with the United States. By opting for the European satellite programme, Germany has thrown in its lot with the French.

This area is only one reflection of the much greater scepticism which French governments have shown in the question of transatlantic economic cooperation. Among all the Europeans, France alone has tried to challenge the US lead in information technology development. France is the most vociferous in trying to defend European entertainments industries against being swamped by American products. Franco-American wrangling on issues such as 'cultural trade' and the trade in agricultural products in the last GATT round was so acrimonious that the talks were thought to have reached an impasse on several occasions. There is clearly, here, a mutual sense of European rivalry which explains some of the underlying tensions between European integration and transatlantic relations.[68]

Chapter 7

An agenda for the twenty-first century

> Today we face the question of what to do to create a
> political institution out of the [North Atlantic] alliance. ...
> I am in favour of an expansion of the military alliance to
> the economic domain and the gradual creation of a common
> Atlantic Market. ... This aim does not contradict the
> unification of Europe but is the continuation of that road.[1]

A new transatlantic treaty?

Proposals for a new transatlantic treaty or a profound reform of NATO
are almost as old as NATO itself.[2] They tended to aim at the inclusion of
new issues into the discussions between Europeans and North Americans. The two Transatlantic Declarations (one between the United States
and the EEC members, the other between Canada and the EEC members)
of November 1990 could be seen as a step in this direction. In October
1992, Chancellor Kohl called for the development of 'links across the
Atlantic' in fields other than defence – in 'politics and economics,
science and cultures'. He expressed the wish that the two Transatlantic
Declarations be translated into 'a comprehensive treaty between Europe
and North America'.[3]

Such ideas were also budding elsewhere. On 30 September 1994,
François Léotard, back from his first NATO meeting as Minister of
Defence, made a plea for a new Atlantic 'partnership'. He noted that
Euro-American relations were institutionalized solely in the area of
defence, in an age when one could expect

> at least a partial disappearance of the cement which the clearly
> perceived common threat constituted. Only the organization

[institutionalization] of the political and economic aspects of the transatlantic relationship will make it possible to avoid their erosion. I therefore think that it is necessary to establish a partnership between, on the one hand, the US and Canada, and on the other, the European Union ...[4]

A fortnight later, British Defence Secretary Malcolm Rifkind, under pressure from Eurosceptic Conservative MPs within the government, launched an initiative for the renewal of the Atlantic Alliance and the strengthening of transatlantic bonds through the creation of an institutionalized Atlantic Community.[5] He made this point several times in 1994–5. At the same conference, the German Defence Minister Volker Rühe also proposed 'a new, wider transatlantic contract', and French Foreign Minister Alain Juppé called for a 'new transatlantic charter to consolidate the common desire of North America and Europe to contribute to international stability in all its dimensions'.[6]

In his Brussels speech of 30 January 1995, Malcolm Rifkind picked up the old idea of an Atlantic Community:

NATO is only a partial expression of Atlantic solidarity; defence and security are only one facet of the interests we share with the North Americans. We need a wider means of expressing the totality of the common interests that bind together Europe and North America, and that make the Atlantic a bridge rather than a gulf.

The 'Atlantic Community' he proposed was not intended, he said,

to echo the European Community nor yet to presage an Atlantic Union. I do mean the sharing of ideas and the promotion of cooperation, consultation and coordination throughout the four pillars of our common interests. In addition to defence and security, there is the rule of law and Parliamentary democracy; liberal capitalism; and our shared European cultural heritage.

Such an Atlantic Community would need to be more than a political statement of common values. It would need underpinning at the institutional level, and by extending to the legislative, economic, business and educational worlds the kinds of regular and deep-seated cooperation that NATO has already brought in the military sphere.[7]

A little later Volker Rühe spoke of a new three-pillar 'transatlantic bargain', comprising political and economic pillars as well as the old security pillar, NATO.[8] In April, Kinkel followed, developing his ideas for a 'Transatlantic Agenda 2000' in a speech given in Chicago: building on the US–European Transatlantic Declaration of 1990, he called for the development of a 'Transatlantic Political Cooperation' mechanism (TAPC), consciously evoking the precedent of European Political Cooperation (the predecessor of the EU's CFSP). This, he argued again, should be complemented by a TAFTA as a further step towards the liberalization of the world market.[9] While France initially showed most reservation with regard to this project – it had had the gravest problems reaching an agreement with the US in GATT, particularly over agriculture and cultural industries – Kinkel attempted to win French support for the TAPC/ TAFTA projects.[10] But it is clear that Kinkel's aim is to move forward both with European integration (particularly moving the CFSP to majority voting) and with the creation of a TAPC and free trade area between the US and the EU.[11] And indeed, by September 1995 even President Jacques Chirac and his Prime Minister Alain Juppé also pronounced in favour of a 'new transatlantic charter'.[12]

There were thus many plans on the table which proposed the strengthening of transatlantic bonds in ways which would go beyond the abolition of tariffs and the restructuring of NATO. They came from many different quarters, most of them European (including French), showing the continuing deep commitment Europeans have to the improvement of transatlantic relations and indeed the widening of formal fora for consultation and agreement to include areas not already covered by NATO.

The Madrid Joint Action Plan

In December 1995, President Clinton met with the leaders of the EU member states in Madrid to agree a Joint Action Plan for future US–EU cooperation. Canada is hoping to be associated with this through a similar agenda it will work out with the EU for the Canadian-EU summit in mid-1996. It emerges from the preparatory discussions that what is sought particularly by the Canadian side is in fact cooperation between the two sides of the Atlantic that shadows the three pillars of the European Union: (1) economic; (2) common foreign and security policy (CFSP); and (3) justice, immigration and international police cooperation. The economic side is addressed by TAFTA plans and hopes for greater cooperation also within the WTO and the G7. The CFSP area

107

would comprise defence, and thus NATO, but should be widened to include political harmonization in areas which have not traditionally been covered by NATO. Cooperation with the EU's third pillar is seen as desirable as the North American countries, and Canada in particular, would like to concert immigration and asylum policy with the EU, and would also like to see cooperation in fighting against drugs and international crime.[13] It is not without irony that these great achievements of the European Union which the Eurosceptics within the EU are doing their best to limit or even reduce are now regarded as attractive areas for cooperation by the North Atlantic powers.

The 'Joint US-EU Action Plan' put forward the broadest agenda yet, founded, predictably, on Wilsonian aims of 'promoting peace and stability, democracy and development around the world'. But it also included the items 'responding to global challenges', 'contributing to the expansion of world trade and closer economic cooperation' and, finally, 'building bridges across the Atlantic'. The list of subheadings in each of these sections is very impressive, as is the fact that the United States has managed to engage the EU on policies on many more issues than the EU has ever known joint actions in its own CFSP. The concrete ways in which this host of issues will be tackled are not outlined in the agenda, however.[14] Nevertheless, the plan gives ground for hope, for it has identified the world's major security problems and economic issues, and has provided the potential basis for the cooperation on these issues between Europe and America which is so vital for their people's security and prosperity, not to mention those of the areas of crisis.

The Joint Action Plan indeed provides a comprehensive agenda for transatlantic cooperation of the sort that the logic of our argument has led us to postulate. It has not, however, specified the formal structures which will enable Europeans and North Americans to achieve these aims through cooperation among themselves and with other countries. The questions surrounding the translation of this agenda into policy, and the innumerable problems which will arise, will occupy the partners on both sides of the Atlantic well into the next century. But at least a start has been made.

Conclusions

The relationship between the North Atlantic countries has been particularly important in international relations since 1941. While the two North American states were involved alongside Britain and France in both the First and Second World Wars, the retreat of the United States into isolationism after the First World War all but severed the security links between the two continents and arguably contributed to the weakness of British and French opposition to the dictators of the Central Axis during the 1930s. Once Hitler, Mussolini and their empires of terror were defeated, it seemed as though the United States might again retreat into its western hemisphere. It was only the perception on both sides of the Atlantic of a huge common threat, posed first by communism as an ideology and then also by the consistently strong Red Army and the armies of the satellite states which were gradually built up by Stalin from 1948, that stopped America's retreat.

This has led many to believe that there was some definitive logical causality between the Soviet threat and America's commitment to Europe; namely, that in the absence of a Soviet threat, the 'normal' policy for the United States would be isolation, or at least a policy in which it is not bound to Europe much more than to any other part of the globe. When first the Warsaw Pact and then the Soviet Union disintegrated, some Europeans believed that the United States would repatriate all its forces in Europe and retreat into bland indifference. On a much smaller scale, the deployment of Canadian forces along the Central Front was ended with the Cold War. Despite their partial redeployment in former Yugoslavia, there was an assumption in Europe that Canada, too, was turning its back on Europe.

Transatlantic bonds seemed to slacken when the GATT disputes seemed more important than the sense of a need for solidarity, a sense which seemed to evaporate when the Soviet Union and its Warsaw Pact disintegrated. Yet the majority of the North Atlantic nations realized that transatlantic ties were more than a tool to contain Soviet communism. They wanted to keep them alive in NATO or in other forms. Even in 1990, governments on both sides of the Atlantic immediately attempted to salvage the relationship by coming forward with Transatlantic Declarations, made jointly in 1990 by Canada and the European Community and then by the United States and the EC, pledging themselves to cooperation and to regular consultation.[15]

The replacement of the GATT negotiation process, which at times had fanned rivalries rather than overcoming them, by the WTO mechanism, was designed to take some of the friction out of this aspect of European–North American relations. More recent proposals for the creation of free trade agreements across the Atlantic go further in this direction.

NATO itself seems to have come out of the doldrums with a new mission to fulfil in securing peace in Bosnia, outside the NATO Treaty area, but not outside Europe. Even the French attitude towards NATO has become more cooperative. But this clearly does not mean that transatlantic relations have gone back to what they were in the Cold War.

The complex and multilayered relations between the Europeans and the North Americans are based essentially on three commonalities: trade, ethnic and cultural kinship, and values. The first, transatlantic trade, is not, in the long term, bound to remain more important than trade between North America and Asia, or between the present EU and East European and North African countries. Quite important developments are possible there. The second is a link that is becoming looser, as immigration from other parts of the world to North America increases, and as US and Canadian cultures become ever more detached from their European ancestry. The common language will remain a strong bond, but only two European states fully share this asset with North America (unless Spain can build on the growing Hispanophony).

The third, the commonality of values, bears in itself greater, universalist aspirations. If the sharing of ideals, particularly basic principles such as democracy, freedom, other human rights, and the faith in free market economics, creates a bond between Europe and North America, then any other country which embraces the same values has an equal right to enter this community. This can apply to eastern Europe, or the many democracies which the retiring empires have left behind, scattered throughout the world, from Australia to South Africa, from India to Brazil. A community based on common, democratic values would be belying its own principles if it turned itself into an exclusive club, denying entry to those who have embraced its ideals. If, however, the key players of that community are downgrading the importance of these values which brought them together as much as did the common threat, then there is little to commend it to allies outside it, and indeed there is little to commend it to some of its own members.

It is also clear that the post-Cold War security challenges affect countries beyond NATO, and indeed should be tackled jointly by the former adversaries, precisely in order to help them lay to rest the old enmity between them. There is no reason why only Washington, London and Paris should worry about WMD proliferation. Moscow, Beijing, Tokyo, Seoul, Rome, Madrid and Bonn are equally concerned, and they should cooperate in enforcing the NPT and other arms control regimes.

Similarly, the major economic challenges affect many countries in the world, and are often truly global challenges – the need to protect the environment, to use the world's limited resources sparingly, to feed its

110

enormously increasing population, and to manage a global economy on the prosperity of which so much depends, if destructive rivalries, friction and even war over resources are to be prevented. Cooperation on a purely North Atlantic basis seems too narrow to tackle all these problems.

At this juncture in world politics, where new antagonisms could easily be built up between the North Atlantic nations and the dynamic Asian economies, where Russia will either become more of a partner or more of an adversary, where China's uncertain future is creating unease in the Far East and Southeast Asia, where long-term problems are unfolding in the world's poorhouses, where terrorism and weapons proliferation can threaten anybody, from any point on the globe, it would be foolish to hope to secure the North Atlantic countries by seeking to insulate them from the rest of the world.

But it will harm no one if the North Atlantic nations preserve their remaining bonds of shared culture and kinship. It would be useful for the stability of Europe and indeed areas beyond it to keep NATO functioning and adapted to new tasks. It could be highly constructive to create new institutions to serve an 'Atlantic Community', in order to confront problems limited to them, or to develop together proposals which could be helpful to wider communities on a global scale. The initiatives that have been put forward on both sides of the Atlantic are thus to be welcomed. In a world of uncertainties, old friends who can be counted upon and share our values are a precious commodity. The Atlantic Community should be preserved and strengthened, not least so that its achievements and values can benefit those beyond it.

In view of the problems facing the North Atlantic nations (and beyond them, many other powers), it is to be welcomed that a new transatlantic agenda is being defined and extended to cover much more than NATO's traditional security tasks.

Yet some clearly contradictory forces are at work, and they are arguably reducing the effectiveness of common efforts. One is the trend back towards nineteenth century concert-of-power behaviour in international relations, with the United States, Britain, France and to a more limited extent Russia among the P5 in the Security Council effectively playing the role of world policemen. This, and even the meetings of the G7 or P8 (the G7 plus Russian), sits oddly with the universalist ideals of the United States, with European integration (which is denied by the exclusion of most EU members and inclusion of others in the P5, G7 and P8), and with the fact that the resources of other North Atlantic nations and indeed other major powers are barely tapped.

Defenders of this development argue that it is only natural that the active 'dirty work' of the post-Cold War era (as opposed to the passive deterrence work of the Cold War) has to be done by those states able and willing to do it, which in itself is the criterion of inequality that distinguishes the United States, Britain and France from the Netherlands, Belgium and Portugal. But it is difficult to see any transatlantic security relationship flourish without the spirit of solidarity, which throughout the Cold War was regarded as vital for NATO, and it is equally difficult to believe that support from smaller European allies (or indeed from Canada) will be strong (or that its absence will not be missed) if they are consistently sidelined.

At the heart of this issue is the future of European integration, which could move towards supranationality at least for those nations which desire it. Only in such a supranational structure would the weight of the smaller powers be used to the full. The creation of such a Europe would offer great advantages for the United States and Canada, as it would be better able to shoulder defence burdens than Britain and France alone. It is crucial that this European integration should not be regarded by powers on either side of the Atlantic as deliberately antagonistic to, or irreconcilable with, transatlantic cooperation, the limits of which must be admitted. The Atlantic Community will not within the foreseeable future move towards supranationality. Supranationality, by contrast, is the logical way of overcoming the bloody national rivalries which have submerged Europe in fratricidal wars in the nineteenth and twentieth centuries. Further European integration, including in the field of defence, is complementary to, not in competition with, transatlantic and indeed more global cooperation.

Given the shared problems and aims of Europeans and North Americans, the projects put forward in order to revitalize transatlantic relations, culminating in the Madrid Action Plan, are clearly steps in the right direction; indeed the Action Plan has identified all the major problems that should be tackled. Implementation, however, will pose problems greater even than those of surviving the Cold War as democracies. It would be truly miraculous if they managed to achieve all the tasks they have set themselves – and yet it is clear that they need to try, not least for their own sake.

We have noted that it may not be in the interest even of the North Atlantic nations, let alone world stability in general, to tackle issues such as non-proliferation or international terrorism and crime merely in the context of a new transatlantic agenda. The United Nations will often offer a more suitable framework within which committees of interested powers could meet to tackle these issues, with further agreement occurring in the G7/P8 and beyond. NATO and any other transatlantic mechanisms yet to be created can underpin policy-making beyond the North Atlantic area, but on their own they are unlikely to be able to resolve the world's new challenges. What is needed in all these fora, however, is the catalyst of a group of 'like-minded' states which have identified common values, and which will work together in applying these values and the resulting interests to the global agenda of contemporary problems. North America and the European Union must be the two poles of a magnet which radiates its shared values throughout the world, until through persuasion and example, and where appropriate through leadership, these values become the underpinning of international order.

Notes

Chapter 1: Introduction

1 They are referred to as such in, for example, 'The Report of the Committee of Three on Non-Military Cooperation in NATO', approved by the North Atlantic Council, 13 December 1956, printed in *NATO Information Service: The North Atlantic Treaty Organisation: Facts and Figures* (Brussels: NATO, 1989), pp. 384–9.

Chapter 2: Transatlantic relations in the past

1 William Pfaff; 'The Allies should get used to the new isolationism', *International Herald Tribune*, 19/20 June 1993.

2 NSC 68 of 1950, item III, published in *Foreign Relations of the United States, 1950*, Vol. I (Washington DC: US Government Printing Office) – henceforth *FRUS* – p. 237 ff.

3 In 1917, and then between 1947 and 1949. See Thomas Etzold and John Lewis Gaddis, *Containment: Documents on American Foreign and Security Policy* (New York: Columbia UP, 1979).

4 Henry Kissinger, *Diplomacy* (New York: Simon & Schuster/Touchstone, 1994), pp. 38–44.

5 Ibid., p. 54.

6 Ibid., p. 46.

7 The Yalta agreement of 1945 has been misrepresented polemically by the French to imply that the United States had sold Eastern Europe 'down the river' to the USSR, when nothing would have been further from the mind of the Wilsonian idealist who was Theodore Roosevelt's nephew Franklin Delano. See Reiner Marcowitz, 'Yalta or the division of the world', in Cyril Buffet and Beatrice Heuser (eds), *Haunted by History: Myths in International relations* (Oxford: Berghahn, forthcoming 1997).

8 NSC 68 of 1950, item III, published in *FRUS*, 1950, Vol. I, p. 237 ff.

9 Harry Cranbrook Allen, *The Anglo-American Relationship since 1783* (London: Adam & Charles Black, 1959), Chapters 1–3.

10 In the traditions of Aristotle, Cicero, Grotius, Pufendorf, Hobbes, Harrington, Burlamanqui, Vattell, Beccaria, Voltaire, Montesquieu and Rousseau, but particularly of Locke.

11 See Alexander Schwan, 'Politische Theorien des Rationalismus und der Aufklärung', in Hans-Joachim Lieber (ed.), *Politische Theorien von der Antike bis zur Gegenwart* (Bonn: Bundeszentrale für Politische Bildung, 1992); Jean-Jacques Chevallier, *Histoire de la pensée politique* (2nd edn, Paris: Payot & Rivages, 1993); Wolfgang Reinhard, 'Vom italienischen Humanismus bis zum Vorabend der Französischen Revolution', and Hans Fenske, 'Politisches Denken von der Französischen Revolution bis zur Gegenwart', in Hans Fenske, Dieter Mertens, Wolfgang Reinhard & Klaus Rosen, *Geschichte der politischen Ideen* (Frankfurt am Main: Fischer, 1987).

12 The Representation of the People Act of 1918 raised this figure to 74% (men above the age of 20 and women above the age of 30). The Representation of the People Act of 1928 finally introduced uniform franchise for men and women of 21 years and over, thus raising the percentage of the population above the age of 20 who could vote to 96.9. Colin F. Padfield, *British Constitution Made Simple* (London: W.H. Allen, 1972), pp. 26–8.

13 The White House, 'A national security strategy of engagement and enlargement' (February 1995), p. 25.

14 Which took the form of the percentages agreement over Eastern Europe he concluded with Stalin in Moscow in December 1944.

15 Catherine McArdle Kelleher, 'US foreign policy and Europe, 1990–2000', *The Brookings Review*, 8/4 (Fall 1990), p. 5 f.

16 NSC 68 of 1950, item III, published in *FRUS*, 1950, Vol. I, p. 237 ff.

17 NSC 7 of May 1948, published in *FRUS,* 1948, Vol. I, p. 546 ff.

18 NSC 20/1, 'US objectives with respect to Russia', 18 August 1948, Liddell Hart Archives, King's College, London, Microfilm No. 71.

19 Belgium, Canada, Denmark, France, Iceland, Italy, Luxembourg, the Netherlands, Norway, Portugal, the United Kingdom, the United States.

20 Christoph Bluth, *Britain, Germany and Western Nuclear Strategy* (Oxford: Clarendon Press, 1995), p. 105 ff.

21 From the original 12, the alliance grew to include Greece and Turkey (1952), the Federal Republic of Germany (1955) and eventually Spain (1976).

22 MORI-Emnid polls of October–November 1994; see 'Germans and British hold similar views on European Union', *Financial Times,* 5 December 1994.

23 John Biggs-Davidson, *The Uncertain Ally* (London: Christopher Johnson, 1957); William Clark, *Less than a Kin: A Study of Anglo-American*

Relations (London: Hamish Hamilton, 1957); Sir Norman Angell, *Defence and the English-speaking Role* (London: Pall Mall Press, 1958); Lionel Morris Gelber, *America in Britain's Place: The Leadership of the West and Anglo-American Unity* (New York: Frederick A. Praeger, 1961); Herbert George Nicholas, *Britain and the United States* (London: Chatto & Windus, 1963); Coral Bell, *The Debatable Alliance: An Essay in Anglo-American Relations* (London: Oxford University Press for the RIIA, 1964); R.B. Manderson-Jones, *The Special Relationship: Anglo-American Relations and Western European Unity, 1947–56* (London: Weidenfeld & Nicolson for the LSE, 1972); Ian S. McDonald (ed.), *Anglo-American Relations since the Second World War* (Newton Abbot: David & Charles, 1974); William Roger Louis and Hedley Bull, *The 'Special Relationship' in Anglo-American Relations since 1945* (Oxford: Clarendon, 1986).

24 Chronologically, not in terms of size.

25 A.J.R. Groom, 'The United States and the British deterrent', *The Yearbook of World Affairs* (London: London Institute of World Affairs) Vol. 18 (1964), p. 73 ff.; John Baylis, *Anglo-American Defence Relations 1939– 1984: The Special Relationship* (2nd edn, London: Macmillan, 1984).

26 John E. Rielly (ed.), *American Public Opinion and U.S. Foreign Policy 1995* (Chicago: Chicago Council on Foreign Relations, 1995), p. 22: on the 'sympathy thermometer' ranging from $0°$ to $80°$ (with $50°$ described as 'neutral feelings'), Britain is given a rating of $69°$, second only to Canada.

27 Macmillan to Richard Crossman, quoted by Anthony Sampson; *Macmillan: A Study in Ambiguity* (London: Allen Lane/Penguin Press, 1967), p. 61.

28 F. S. Northedge, *The Troubled Giant: Britain among the Great Powers, 1916-1939* (London: Bell & Son for the London School of Economics and Political Science, 1966), pp. 618-22.

29 Cf. Simon Duke, *US Defence Bases in the United Kingdom: A Matter for Joint Decision?* (London: Macmillan for St Antony's College, Oxford, 1987).

30 Raymond Seitz, 'The Anglo-American relationship', Speech to the Royal Institute of International Affairs, 23 March 1993, distributed by USIS.

31 Raymond Seitz's valedictory address, made in spring 1994, was less equivocal, but the former, not the latter, message is heard more often.

32 Most recently perhaps by Ian Davidson, 'A hollow shell', *Financial Times,* 28 June 1995.

33 The crucial differences lie in France's adoption of ideals of social welfare and in differing economic concepts, France believing in a greater degree of state interference and protectionism.

34 Jacques Chirac in *Le Monde,* 1 February 1996.

35 'Discours du Président de la République, M. Jacques Chirac, devant le Congrès des Etats-Unis d'Amérique', Washington DC, 1 February 1996, *Statements* SFC/96/32.

36 See for example Pompidou's speeches during his visit to the United States in February 1970: 'Jamais nous ne sommes entrés en conflit avec les Etats-Unis', *Le Monde,* 26 February 1970; 'Text of address by President Pompidou', *New York Times,* 26 February 1970.

37 Jacques Amalric and André Passeron, 'Le conseil des ministres fait le bilan', *Le Monde,* 5 March 1970.

38 General André Beaufre, *NATO and Europe,* trans. Joseph Green (New York: Vintage Books, 1966), p. vii.

39 'Discours du Président de la République. *Statements,* SFC/96/32.

40 Alfred Grosser, *The Western Alliance: European–American Relations since 1945* trans. Michael Shaw (London: Macmillan, 1980), pp. 4–6; Michel Winock: '"US go home": l'antiaméricanisme français', *L'Histoire,* No. 50 (November 1982), pp. 7–20.

41 The Minitel story illustrates this point. This very competitive rival to the Internet was marketed and popularized in France long before the Internet found customers in other European countries. Yet the language barrier of the francophone Minitel network made it unattractive for export, and France's bid to create an ingenious and low-cost alternative to the US-dominated Internet showed only temporary returns. Users in France, too, are now turning to the American net.

42 'M. Giscard d'Estaing: la France doit avoir une capacité militaire propre mobile ...', *Le Monde,* 10–11 November 1974; 'Pour la première fois, Valéry Giscard d'Estaing', *Le Figaro,* 12 November 1975.

43 Alexandre Sanguinetti, quoted in Jean d'Ormesson: 'Nos amis américains', *Revue des deux Mondes,* 145/1 (January 1974), p. 9.

44 Thierry Maulnier (of the Académie Française), 'L'antiaméricanisme et les Américains', *La Revue des deux Mondes,* 145/3 (March 1975), p. 523.

45 Philippe de Saint-Robert, 'La France contre les Etats-Unis', *Combat,* 11 August 1967.

46 John W. Young, *France, the Cold War and the Western Alliance, 1944-1949* (Leicester: Leicester University Press, 1990), pp. 198–221.

47 Maurice Vaïsse, 'Aux origines du mémorandum de septembre 1958', *Relations Internationales,* 58 (Summer 1989).

48 Ernst Weisenfeld, 'Les grandes lignes de la politique etrangère de la France', *Politique étrangère* 40/1 (January 1975), p. 6.

49 Pierre Mélandri, 'La France et les Etats-Unis', *Politique étrangère* 51/1 (Spring 1986), p. 223.

50 Beatrice Heuser, 'Future trends in British, French and German defence and security policy', in Ann-Sofie Dahl (ed.), *Security in Our Time* (Stockholm: FOA, 1995).

51 Beatrice Heuser, 'Mitterrand's Gaullism: Cold-War policies for post-Cold War world?', in Antonio Varsori (ed.), *Europe 1945-1989: The End of an Era* (New York: St Martin's Press, 1994), pp. 346–69.

52   Michel Tatu, 'Tangage franco-américain', *Le Monde,* 29 May 1992;
     François de Rose, 'Must U.S.–French tensions be eternal?', *International
     Herald Tribune,* 17 June 1992; Roger Cohen, 'U.S.-French ties: the big
     chill', *International Herald Tribune,* 2 July 1992; Pierre Lellouche,
     'Défense: divisions Franco-Américaines', *Le Point,* 10 October 1992.
53   Rielly (ed.), *American Public Opinion and U.S. Foreign Policy 1995,*
     p. 22.
54   David S. Yost, 'France and the Gulf War of 1990-1991: political-military
     lessons learned', *Journal of Strategic Studies,* 16/3 (September 1993),
     pp. 339–74.
55   Jean Quatremer, 'Paris noue le dialogue nucléaire à l'Otan', *Libération,* 17
     January 1996.
56   'Discours du Président de la République', *Statements,* SFC/96/32.
57   In March 1991, France associated itself with the work within NATO that
     led to the definition of the new NATO strategy, adopted in November 1991.
     See Philippe Lemaître, 'La France participera désormais aux travaux du
     Comité des plans de la défense de l'OTAN', *Le Monde,* 19 March 1991;
     Claire Tréan, 'France-OTAN: le chat et la souris', *Le Monde,* 4 May 1991.
58   Collectively, Irish, Scottish and other British descendants are more
     numerous, but it is worth remembering that descendants from Irish,
     Scottish and Welsh immigrants are likely to be anti-English, and there is
     thus no collective Anglo-Saxon bond tying all Americans of British/Irish
     descent to the United Kingdom. See below.
59   Ex-Prime Minister Thatcher noted in her memoirs that from the beginning
     of the Bush presidency in January 1989, she was facing 'an administration
     which saw Germany as its main European partner in leadership ... I felt I
     could not always rely as before on American co-operation'. See Margaret
     Thatcher, *Downing Street Years* (London: HarperCollins, 1993), p. 768.
     See also Pierre Briançon, 'Clinton redessine l'Europe autour de
     l'Allemagne', *Libération,* 12 July 1994; Roger Boyes, 'Clinton enhances
     Bonn's role on world stage', *The Times,* 12 July 1994.
60   Rielly (ed.), *American Public Opinion and U.S. Foreign Policy 1995,* p. 22.
61   'A new NATO', *The Economist,* 9 December 1995.
62   'España culmina su proceso de integración en la OTAN', *El Pais,* 6 July
     1994.
63   See the report by the Netherlands government to the Netherlands Parlia-
     ment, *'The Common European Foreign, Security and Defence Policy:
     Ways to Strengthen the European Union's Ability to Act Externally',*
     March 1995.
64   MORI-Emnid polls of October–November 1994 (see note 22 above).
65   Lawrence Freedman, 'Europe waits for reluctant giant to take lead',
     Independent, 7 January 1994; Martin Lambeck, 'Europa braucht starkes
     Amerika', *Die Welt,* 1 February 1994.

66 Richard Holbrooke, 'America, a European power', *Foreign Affairs*, 74/2 (February 1995), pp. 38–50.
67 Jenonne Walker, 'Keeping America in Europe', *Foreign Policy*, 83 (Summer 1991), p. 129.
68 North America Department, Foreign and Commonwealth Office, 'Atlantic Fellowships in public policy', press announcement (3 February 1995).
69 Based on interviews conducted with US and Canadian students at King's College and the London School of Economic, both parts of the University of London, and at the University of Oxford, 1981–96.
70 US Bureau of the Census, *1990 Census of Population and Housing Data Paper Listing* (CPD-L-133), and US Bureau of the Census, *Statistical Abstract of the United States: 1994* (Washington, DC, 1995), p. 18.

Chapter 3: Canada: a transatlantic hinge

1 Government Statement, *Canada in the World* (Ottawa, 1995), p. 34.
2 For a very level-headed, intelligent summary and analysis, see Denis Stairs, 'Contemporary security issues', in Special Joint Committee Reviewing Canadian Foreign Policy (ed.), *Canada's Foreign Policy: Position Papers* (Ottawa: Parliamentary Publications Directorate, 1994), pp. 6–8.
3 Ibid., p. 8.
4 Government Statement: *Canada in the World* (Hull: Canadian International Development Service, 1995), pp. 34–36.
5 John E. Rielly (ed.), *American Public Opinion and U.S. Foreign Policy 1995*, p. 22: on the 'sympathy thermometer', Canada is attributed the highest figure at 73°.
6 The text of the referendum was as follows:
   The Government of Quebec has made public its proposal to negotiate a new agreement with the rest of Canada, based on the equality of nations; this agreement would enable Quebec to acquire the exclusive powers to make its laws, levy its taxes and establish relations abroad – in other words, sovereignty – and at the same time, to maintain with Canada an economic association including a common currency; no change in political status resulting from these negotiations will be effected without approval from the people through another referendum; on these terms, do you give the Government of Quebec the mandate to negotiate the proposed agreement between Quebec and Canada?
   See Kenneth McNaught, *The Penguin History of Canada* (4th edn, London and Harmondsworth: Penguin Books, 1988), p. 340.
7 Gordon Mace, Louis Bélanger and Ivan Bernier, 'Canadian foreign policy and Quebec', in Maxwell A. Cameron and Maureeen Appel Molot (eds), *Canada among Nations 1995: Democracy and Foreign Policy* (Ottawa: Carleton University Press, 1995), pp. 119–44.

8 The text this time read:
Do you agree that Quebec should become sovereign after having made a formal offer to Canada for a new economic and political partnership, within the scope of the bill respecting the future of Quebec and of the agreement signed on June 12, 1995?

9 'Parizeau makes way for Bouchard', and David Usborne, 'Province is left more divided than ever', *Independent,* 1 November 1995; Sylviane Tramier, 'Les indépendantistes québécois rejettent la proposition d'Ottawa de faire de leur province une "société distincte"', *Le Monde,* 14 December 1995.

10 Michael Hart with Bill Dymond and Colin Robertson, *Decision at Midnight: Inside the Canada–US Free-Trade Negotiations* (Vancouver: University of British Columbia Press, 1994), pp. 107–14.

11 Interviews conducted in Ottawa and Toronto, 10–13 December 1996.

12 Sylviane Tramier, 'Le premier ministre canadien remanie son gouvernement', *Le Monde,* 27 January 1996; Clyde H. Farnsworth, 'Quebec's Premier eases the tension', *International Herald Tribune,* 9 April 1996.

13 Special Joint Committee Reviewing Canadian Foreign Policy, *Canada's Foreign Policy: Principles and Priorities for the Future,* p. 54; *Canada, National Defence: 1994 Defence White Paper* (Ottawa: Canada Supply and Communication Group, 1994), pp. 9–11.

14 Denis Stairs, 'Contemporary security issues', in Special Joint Committee Reviewing Canadian Foreign Policy (ed.), *Canada's Foreign Policy: Position Papers*, p. 6.

Chapter 4: The security context

1 The White House, 'A national security strategy of engagement and enlargement', February 1995, p. 1.

2 'Discours du Président de la République, M. Jacques Chirac, devant le Congrès des Etats-Unis d'Amérique', Washington, DC, 1 February 1996, *Statements,* SFC/96/32.

3 This argument has most recently been made by Paul-Marie de la Gorce: 'Retour honteux de la France dans l'OTAN', *Le Monde Diplomatique,* January 1996.

4 Beatrice Heuser and Georges Tan Eng Bok, 'OTAN: Continuité et évolution', *Défense Nationale,* 47th year (December 1991), pp. 105–14.

5 Beatrice Heuser, 'L'avenir de la sécurité en Europe', *Défense Nationale,* 47th year (April 1991), pp. 53–66.

6 The White House, 'A national security strategy of engagement and enlargement', p. 23.

7 With the exception of the 1948–55 period, when the Americans in particular were thoroughly active trying to subvert communist regimes; cf.

Bennet Kovrig, *The Myth of Liberation* (Baltimore, MD: Johns Hopkins University Press, 1973), and Beatrice Heuser, 'Covert action within British and American concepts of containment, 1944–51', in Richard Aldrich (ed.), *British Intelligence, Strategy and the Cold War, 1945–51* (London: Routledge, 1992).

8 Indeed, it might even stand to benefit Russia, making its association with the EU through an agreement similar to that recently concluded with Turkey a possibility.

9 'US role in Council of Europe', *Financial Times,* 11 January 1996.

10 Cf. Beatrice Heuser, *Strategies in Europe since 1945: Towards a European Nuclear Force?* (London: Macmillan, forthcoming), Chapter 1.

11 Tom Rhodes, 'Russia halts nuclear talks as relations with US cool', *The Times,* 22 January 1996.

12 See IISS, *Strategic Survey 1994–1995* (Oxford: Oxford University Press, 1995), pp. 25–51.

13 Martin Navias, *Ballistic Missile Proliferation in the Third World,* Adelphi Papers 252 (London: IISS, Summer 1990); see also Peter van Ham, *Managing Non-Proliferation Regimes in the 1990s,* Chatham House Paper (London: Pinter for the RIIA, 1993).

14 'NATO's response to proliferation of weapons of mass destruction', Press Release (95)124 of 29 November 1995, p. 3.

15 See, e.g., Ambassador Henry F. Cooper, Director, Strategic Defense Initiative Organization, Speech to the Committee on Armed Services of the US Senate, 20 June 1991, typescript made available by the US Embassy, Paris; President Bush's State of the Union Message, 28 January 1992, USIS, p. 4.

16 Warren Christopher and William Perry, 'A bill to maim American foreign policy', *International Herald Tribune* 14 February 1995; see also 'Senate passes plan for missile defense: measures revised over issue of ABM treaty provisions', *International Herald Tribune,* 7 September 1995.

17 'Russians question nuclear treaty', *International Herald Tribune,* 30 January 1996; Tom Rhodes, 'Russia halts nuclear talks as relations with US cool', *The Times,* 22 January 1996; 'Russians question nuclear treaty', *International Herald Tribune,* 30 January 1996.

18 NATO doctrine since the Ottawa Meeting of the North Atlantic Council in 1974.

19 There is a certain margin of what could be done with stand-off weapons, or low-flying sea-launched ballistic missiles, but even here, an ABM shield, depending on its properties, would most probably be a complicating factor.

20 There are indications, however, that the United States has worked on nuclear deterrence concepts aimed at potential nuclear proliferators: Eric Schmitt, 'U.S. is redefining nuclear deterrence: terrorist nations targeted', *International Herald Tribune,* 26 February 1993.

Notes

21 'Aspin outlines new "counter-proliferation" policy', Speech by Secretary of Defense Les Aspin to the National Academy of Sciences on 7 December 1993, USIS (9 December 1993); 'Davis outlines U.S. nonproliferation policy', Under-Secretary of State for International Security and Arms Control Lynn Davis before the Atlantic Council, 8 December 1994, USIS (14 December 1994).

22 Gregory Fox, 'The UN as state-builder', in Sohail Hashmi (ed.), *State Sovereignty; Change and Persistence in International Relations* (Philadelphia: Pennsylvania University Press, forthcoming 1997).

23 In the case of the UN, it was mainly the United States which found fault with proceedings. There is a curious phenomenon emerging in the current hostility shown by sections of the US administration towards the UN and its working: here is arguably a rival candidate for world leadership, something that is difficult to reconcile with US self-perception, with its reluctance to put its forces under the command of non-American officers.

24 Boutros Boutros-Ghali, *An Agenda for Peace* (New York, United Nations, July 1992).

25 IWF, *World Economic Outlook 1995*, data quoted in Mario v. Baratta (ed.), *Der Fischer Weltalmanach 96* (Frankfurt/Main: Fischer Taschenbuch Verlag, 1995), p. 943.

26 Germany's net payment into the EU in 1994 was DM21.2 billion, as against Britain's net equivalent of DM4.3 billion, and France's of DM1.7 billion – *Handelsblatt,* quoted in Mario v. Baratta (ed.), *Der Fischer Weltalmanach '96,* p. 917. (Billion is used throughout in the American sense.)

27 SINUS and Friedrich Ebert Foundation for STERN, *Sowjetische und amerikanischen Politik im Urteil der Deutschen in der Bundesrepublik* (Munich: SINUS, 1988), p. 64.

28 Asmus, *Germany's Geopolitical Maturation*, p. 22 (see Table 4.1 above).

29 Bernhard Fleckenstein and Hans-Georg Räder, *Die neue deutsche Sicherheitspolitik im Meinungsbild der Bevölkerung SOWI Arbeitspapier Nr. 73* (Munich: Sozialwissenschaftliches Institut der Bundeswehr, January 1993), pp. 11, 44.

30 France and Belgium, coming second and third as recipients of German foreign investment at DM25.8 billion and DM25.1 billion respectively, thus receive roughly a third each of what the United States gets. Next come Britain and the Netherlands with DM19.2 billion and DM18.3 billion respectively, followed by Ireland (DM14.7 billion), Spain (DM13.7 billion), Italy (DM12.9 billion), Switzerland (DM11.3 billion), Austria (DM11.3 billion) and Luxemburg (DM10.4 billion). Then come Brazil (DM9.2 billion), Canada (DM7.1 billion) and Japan (DM5.9 billion), leaving DM36.8 billion for all other recipients. Globus statistics: 'Kapital ins Ausland', *Süddeutsche Zeitung,* 23 June 1994.

31 Ronald D. Asmus, *German Strategy and Opinion After the Wall, 1990–1993* (Santa Monica, CA: RAND for the Friedrich Naumann Foundation, 1994), p. 25.

32 Asmus, *Germany in Transition*, p. 34 (see Table 4.1 above); Asmus, *Germany's Geopolitical Maturation*; Fleckenstein and Räder: *Die neue deutsche Sicherheitspolitik*, pp. 3, 5. See also Philip H. Gordon, 'The normalization of German foreign policy', *Orbis* (Spring 1994), pp. 225–43.

33 Joseph Fitchett, 'Germans warming to use of soldiers on global mission', *International Herald Tribune*, 8 February 1995.

34 'Germany's Greens inch away from absolute pacifism', *International Herald Tribune*, 4 December 1995.

35 Elizabeth Pond, 'Germany's emerging consensus on out-of-area missions', *Wall Street Journal*, 28 June 1995.

36 Günther Nolting, 'Der schwierige Marsch der Hardthöhe ins dritte Jahrtausend', *Die Welt*, 6 October 1995.

37 Bundesministerium der Verteidigung, *Weißbuch 1994: Weißbuch zur Sicherheit der Bundesrepublik Deutschland und zur Lage und Zukunft der Bundeswehr* (Bonn, 1994), pp. 42–5.

38 'Grüne lehnen Bundeswehr-Einsatz in Ostslawonien ab', *Süddeutsche Zeitung*, 8 February 1996; Frank Müller, 'Meinungsforschung prophezeit der SPD eine Katastrophe', *Süddeutsche Zeitung*, 8 January 1996.

39 Asmus, *Germany's Geopolitical Maturation*.

40 Emma Matanle, *The UN Security Council: Prospects for Reform*, Discussion Paper No. 62 (London: RIIA, 1995).

41 'U.S. supports Germany, Japan for Security Council', USIS Wireless File, 10 June 1993.

42 For example, German concerns about the large numbers of refugees sheltering in Germany have on a number of occasions led to violence against refugees by extremist youth groups; in other contexts German neighbours have listened with anxiety to domestic rhetoric addressed to the organizations of former German refugees from the East.

43 René H. Cuperus: 'Gefährlicher Alleingang: die SPD wird zum Problemkind in Europa', *Die Zeit*, 12 January 1996.

44 Having spent most of the period of the Third Reich in a concentration camp, Kurt Schumacher was singularly immune to the feelings of guilt which other Germans developed about the National-Socialist period. He strongly campaigned for German unification at the time of the founding of the Federal Republic and the Democratic Republic.

45 Karsten Voigt: 'Plädoyer für eine zivile NATO', *Internationale Politik*, 30/12 (December 1995).

46 Four-plus-Two Treaty on German Union, Article 3(1) of 12 September 1990.

47 Statement issued by the North Atlantic Council Meeting in Ministerial

Session in Copenhagen on 6/7 June 1991, Press Communiqué M-1(91)42, p. 3.

48 'The situation in the Soviet Union', Statement issued by the North Atlantic Council meeting in Ministerial Session at NATO Headquarters, Brussels (21 August 1991), Press Communiqué M-2(91)60.

49 German Foreign Office Press Communiqué 1212/91, 'Erklärung des Bundesminister des Auswärtigen Hans-Dietrich Genscher und des amerikanischen Aussenministers James A. Baker III', 2 October 1991.

50 'MM Havel, Walesa et Antall demandent une forme d'association avec l'OTAN', *Le Monde*, 8 October 1991.

51 Joseph Fitchett, 'NATO must prepare to open membership to the East, US says', *International Herald Tribune*, 8 November 1991.

52 NATO Information Service, 'NATO Partnership for Peace', Brussels, 10 January 1994.

53 'Study on NATO enlargement', G/PA/NC/PO/95/177 of 28 September 1995.

54 See for example Ronald Asmus, Richard Kugler and F. Stephen Larrabee, 'Building a new NATO', *Foreign Affairs*, 72/4 (September 1993); Friedbert Pflueger, 'Take PFP one step further', *Wall Street Journal Europe*, 6 July 1994.

55 See for example Gunther Hellmann and Rheinhard Wolf, 'Don't build on shaky foundations', *International Herald Tribune*, 18 September 1993.

56 'Streamlining NATO', *International Herald Tribune*, 3 June 1991.

57 'US outlines military cuts across Europe', *Wall Street Journal*, 30 March 1993.

58 Craig Whitney, 'Troop cut in Europe draws concern – General says U.S. must keep 65,000 soldiers in Germany', *International Herald Tribune*, 4 August 1993.

59 Les Aspin, 'Forces and alliances for a new era', Speech in Brussels, 12 September 1993.

60 Pierre Lellouche, 'Otan: le rendez-vous manqué', *Le Figaro*, 11 January 1994.

61 Clyde Farnsworth, 'Canada to pull out all forces in Europe', *International Herald Tribune*, 28 February 1992.

62 'NATO seeks from Canada assurance on Alliance role', *International Herald Tribune*, 25 March 1992.

63 Martin du Bois, 'Rush to cut military leaves NATO's plans for Europe in disarray', *Wall Street Journal*, 22 January 1993.

64 NATO Office of Information and Press, Basic Fact Sheet No. 5 (September 1993), 'NATO's new force structures'.

65 For preliminary US studies, see US Secretary of Defense, Report to Congress, 'Report on allied contributions to the common defense' (1995), p. III–7.; US Secretary of Defense, Report to Congress, 'Toward a new partnership in responsibility sharing', April 1995.

66 Michael Gordon, 'US military may take wars one at a time', *International Herald Tribune,* 31 May 1993.

67 'Aspin: US reviewing responses to military threat', Speech to NATO Defence University (17 June 1993), USIS; 'Aspin spells out further proposed cuts in US military', Speech at Georgetown University on Bottom-Up Review (2 September 1993), USIS.

68 Paul Horvitz, 'U.S. foresees a tight but highly lethal military force – 5 year strategy seeks capability of winning simultaneous conflicts', *International Herald Tribune,* 2 September 1993; see also the White House, 'A national security strategy of engagement and enlargement', February 1995, pp. 3, 9.

69 Warren Christopher and William Perry, 'A bill to maim American foreign policy', *International Herald Tribune,* 14 February 1995; see also 'Talbott on US–European interdependence', Deputy Secretary of State's speech at State Department, 5 October 1995, USIS.

70 Christopher Bellamy, 'Pentagon forced to rethink its world strategy', *Independent,* 20 September 1995.

71 A buzzword employed by Ronald D. Asmus, Richard L. Kugler and Stephen Larrabee, 'It's time for a new US–European strategic bargain', *International Herald Tribune,* 28–29 August 1993.

72 Georges-Henri Soutou, 'La sécurité de la France dans l'après-guerre'; Pierre Guillen, 'Les militaires français et la création de l'OTAN', and Pierre Gerbet, 'Le rôle de la France dans la négociation', in Maurice Vaïsse, Pierre Mélandri and Frédéric Bozo (eds), *La France et l'OTAN, 1949–1996* (Brussels: Complexe, 1996).

73 Maurice Vaïsse, 'Indépendance et solidarité', in *La France et l'OTAN.*

74 Nicholas Doughty, 'NATO, under landmark accord, will adopt peacekeeping role outside its boundaries', *Wall Street Journal,* 22 May 1992. See also the Final Communiqué of the Defence Planning and Nuclear Planning Group Meeting, M-DPC/NPG-1(92)44 of 27 May 1992.

75 Claire Tréan, 'L'élargissement des compétences de l'OTAN continue d'alimenter la polémique entre Français et Américains', *Le Monde,* 6 June 1992; see also Bernt Conrad, 'Frankreich will Nato nicht zur KSZE-Truppe aufwerten', *Die Welt,* 4 July 1992.

76 Joseph Fitchett, 'NATO readies an airlift for relief of Sarajevo', *International Herald Tribune,* 27–28 June 1992.

77 'Die Nato bereitet sich auf friedenserhaltende Missionen vor', *Frankfurter Allgemeine Zeitung,* 21 October 1992.

78 Beatrice Heuser, 'Jugoslawien: Labor für Experimente in der Europäischen Sicherheit', *Europäische Sicherheit,* 4 (1993), pp. 194–6.

79 Stéphanie Marchand, 'Washington-Paris: nouvelle donne', *Le Figaro,* 23 February 1994.

80 Pierre Lefèvre, 'Pagaille dans l'Alliance atlantique', *Le Soir,* 29 November 1994; see also Nicholas Timmins, 'US move "signals end of Nato"',

Independent, 14 November 1994; Jeane Kirkpatrick, 'The Euro-American Alliance weakens', *International Herald Tribune,* 25 November 1994; Bruce Clark and Bernard Gray, 'United front splinter', *Financial Times,* 30 May 1995.

81 Elizabeth Wood, 'Alliance breaks new ground', *European Voice,* 24 November 1995.

82 Doubts were expressed e.g. by William Pfaff: 'Europe must learn to manage without American assistance', *International Herald Tribune,* 20 January 1996; Kurt Kister: 'Die lustlose Weltmacht', *Süddeutsche Zeitung,* 5–7 January 1996.

83 Andrew Marshall, 'Nato seeks to bring France into the fold', *Independent,* 15 November 1993; Peter Gumbel, 'NATO summit is set to allow West Europe independent defense', *Wall Street Journal,* 11 January 1994.

84 'Declaration of the heads of state and government participating in the meeting of the North Atlantic Council held at NATO headquarters, Brussels' (10-11 January 1994), NATO Press Communiqué M-1(94)3, p. 6.

85 NATO Press communiqué M-NAC-1(96)63 of 3 June 1996.

86 This is not to say that under Article 5, any NATO member is committed to a specific form of action. But in the Cold War, the deployment of forces in the integrated military structure would have made it more complicated – yet not impossible – for an individual country, particularly along the Central Front, not to take action as planned together with its allies.

87 Article 5 obligations are formulated as the intrinsic right to self-defence, including collective self-defence, by any member of the UN or group of members organized in a regional defence association based on the Charter of the UN. It is true, however, that nothing can force a member of NATO even under an Article 5 case to take any particular action in defence of its NATO partners.

88 See the Bertelsmann Foundation's 'CFSP and the future of the European Union', July 1995.

89 Cf. US Secretary of Defense, Report to Congress: 'Report on allied contributions to the common defense' (1995), p. III–7; US Secretary of Defense, Report to Congress, 'Toward a new partnership in responsibility sharing', April 1995.

Chapter 5: The Age of Mercury

1 Cf. Susan Strange, *States and Markets* (2nd edn, London: Pinter, 1994), pp. 43–138.

2 Presse- und Informationsamt der Bundesregierung, *Bulletin* No. 93, 10 November 1995, p. 908.

3 'Federalism', both in the US and German political contexts, means the devolving of power in certain spheres (such as foreign and defence policies) to a central government while ensuring the retention of other powers (culture, local economics) on a lower (state, *Land*) level. The opposite tendency in the US, the anti-federalist tradition, stems from a tradition of distrust in central government, shared with anarchist traditions. In a strongly centralized state such as France, 'federalism' comes to be coterminous with the movement for the decentralization of the state. But given the current looseness of European integration, the proponents of 'federalism' aspire to greater centralization within the EU.

4 Vera Graaf, 'Sovereign Citizens', *Süddeutsche Zeitung,* 13 October 1995.

5 Cf. Ronald E. Powaski, *The Entangling Alliance: The United States and European Security, 1950–1993* (Westport, CT: Greenwood Press, 1994), pp. 57–114.

6 'Overdoing it on defense', *International Herald Tribune,* 11 July 1995; 'Senate passes plan for missile defense', *International Herald Tribune,* 7 September 1995; Stephen Rosenfeld, 'When it comes to defense, America lacks a coherent strategy', *International Herald Tribune,* 20 November 1995.

7 Simon Jenkins, 'When old friends fall out', *Independent,* 5 December 1994.

8 Jonathan Freedland, 'Angry Rifkind scolds critics in Congress', *Guardian,* 22 June 1995.

9 In June 1995, British Defence Secretary Malcolm Rifkind travelled to Washington and tried to meet Congressmen and women at a lunch arranged in the Congress building, and only a negligible fraction of those invited deigned to attend. See Jim Mann, 'Post-Cold War generation on Capitol Hill questions tie to NATO', *International Herald Tribune,* 4 December 1995. In February 1996, French President Chirac addressed a Congressional meeting which was poorly attended, ostensibly because of a boycott of French nuclear tests, which had, however, by then been concluded.

10 Josef Joffe, 'Atlantische Probescheidung', *Süddeutsche Zeitung,* 25 November 1993; Peter Hort, 'Eine Ehe kommt in die Jahre', *Frankfurter Allgemeine,* 14 June 1995; Klaus-Dieter Frankenberger, 'Interessen und Vertrauen', *Frankfurter Allgemeine,* 4 October 1995.

11 Cf. John E. Rielly (ed.), *American Public Opinion and U.S. Foreign Policy 1995,* p. 15.

12 For the significant shift to domestic concerns and the gap between public opinion and elite opinion in the US, see also Rielly, *American Public Opinion and U.S. Foreign Policy 1995,* pp. 31, 35, 39.

13 John Eisenhammer, 'US warns trade dispute could imperil NATO', *Independent,* 10 February 1992; Ian Murray, 'US threatens to abandon

Nato over trade talks', *The Times,* 10 February 1992; David Gow, 'Gatt impasse threatens Nato alliance, warns US', *Guardian,* 10 February 1992.

14 'Cool winds from the White House', *The Economist,* 27 March 1993.

15 James F. Dobbins, US Ambassador to the European Union; 'Uncertainties of US–European relations', Speech of 4 March 1993, European Wireless File.

16 Sir Leon Brittan, Vice-President of the Eurupean Commission, speech to the American Club of Brussels, 27 April 1995: 'The EU–US Relationship: will it last?', paper provided by the European Commission.

17 Figures supplied by the US Department of Commerce for 1994.

18 Speech by US Secretary of State James A. Baker to the Berlin Press Club, 14 December 1989, USIS.

19 Ambassador James F. Dobbins, 'Europe and America in the post-Cold War era: agenda for a Euro-Atlantic Community', speech given to the Centre for European Policy Studies, Brussels, 24 May 1993.

20 François Léotard, 'La sécurité européenne', *Le Figaro,* 30 September 1994.

21 'Christopher cites key principles, agenda for foreign policy', speech to the Kennedy School of Government, 20 January 1995, USIS.

22 Sir Leon Brittan, 'The EU–US Relationship: will it last?'

23 Presse- und Informationsamt der Bundesregierung: *Bulletin* No. 12 (16 February 1995), p. 98; see also Klaus Kinkel, 'Germany sets an evolving agenda for a still much needed alliance', *International Herald Tribune,* 30 March 1995.

24 The Hon. Roy MacLaren, 'The Occident Express: towards transatlantic free trade', speech to the Royal Institute of International Affairs, 22 May 1995.

25 See e.g. the address by Jean-Pierre Juneau, Assistant Deputy Minister for Europe, Department of Foreign Affairs and International Trade to the sixth Canada-Germany symposium, Montreal, 16 November 1995, text made available by Canadian Department of Foreign Affairs.

26 See, e.g, Alan M. Rugman, *Multinationals and Canada–United States Free Trade* (Columbia: University of South Carolina Press, 1990); Alan M. Rugman, 'A Canadian perspective on NAFTA', *International Executive,* 36/1 (January–February 1994), pp. 33–54; Michael Gestrin and Alan M. Rugman, 'The strategic response of multinational enterprises to NAFTA', *Columbia Journal of World Business* (Winter 1993), pp. 18–29.

27 The term 'globalization' of the world economy has begun to be used to describe the marked increase of foreign direct investment since the 1980s.

28 Speech by Douglas Hurd to the Economic Club, Chicago, 18 May 1995, text made available by the British Foreign Office.

29 Speech by the Foreign Secretary, Malcolm Rifkind, to the Transatlantic Policy Network, Queen Elizabeth II Conference Centre, London, 6 February 1996, text made available by the Canadian High Commission.

30 See also the address by Roy MacLaren, Minister for International Trade of

Canada, to the Canada-UK Chamber of Commerce, Ironmongers' Hall, 23 January 1996, text made available by the Canadian High Commission.

Chapter 6: Atlanticism vs. European integration?

1 Charles de Gaulle, Note of 17 July 1961, *Lettres, notes et carnets* (Paris: Plon, 1980).

2 On the early history of US encouragement of European integration, see Pascaline Winand, *Eisenhower, Kennedy and the United States of Europe* (London: Macmillan, 1994).

3 Geir Lundestad, '"Empire" by integration: the United States and European integration, 1945–1996', in Kathleen Burk and Melvyn Leffler (eds), *The United States and Europe since 1945* (London: forthcoming, 1997).

4 Message of Helmut Kohl and François Mitterrand to President of the European Council Andreotti, 6 December 1990, *Bulletin d'Information*, 10 December 1990, and see Alan Riding, 'Paris and Bonn offer EC security plan', *International Herald Tribune,* 8 December 1990.

5 'London lehnt deutsch-französischen Plan ab', *Süddeutsche Zeitung*, 6 February 1991; Reuters: 'EC to discuss defence with Western European Union', 14 February 1991; 'Neues Konzept für WEU: London gegen Einbau des Militärbündnisses in die EG', *Süddeutsche Zeitung*, 28/29 March 1991.

6 Joseph Fitchett, 'France and U.S. bridge a gulf', *International Herald Tribune,* 14 March 1991.

7 'Nouvel avertissement des Etats-Unis aux Douze à propos de la défense européenne', *Le Monde,* 2 May 1991; William Pfaff, 'America could stand to brush up on the language of partnership', *International Herald Tribune,* 17 May 1991.

8 Philippe Lemaître, 'Les désaccords à propos d'une politique de défense européenne restent entiers', *Le Monde,* 30 April 1991.

9 Claire Tréan, 'L'OTAN reconnaît à l'Europe des Douze le droit de se doter d'une politique de sécurité', *Le Monde,* 9/10 June 1991.

10 'Quatre mille deux cents hommes en cinq garnisons', *Le Monde,* 17 October 1991.

11 Christian d'Epenoux, 'Böblingen: naissance d'une armée', *L'Express,* 31 October 1991.

12 In July 1990 President Mitterrand announced the complete withdrawal of all French forces from the Federal Republic, assuming that on reunification, Germany would be asking its 'occupation forces' to withdraw. It was pointed out to him, however, that in December 1966, after France's withdrawal from the military integration of NATO, Bonn secured a commitment from Paris to leave French forces in the Federal Republic. Cf. '"La logique voudra que l'armée française stationnée en Allemagne

regagne son pays" déclare M. Mitterrand', *Le Monde*, 8–9 June 1990;
see 'Deutsch-französische Regierungsvereinbarung über das
Stationierungsrecht der französischen Truppen in der Bundesrepublik
Deutschland vom 21. Dezember 1966', Auswärtiges Amt (ed.), *40 Jahre
Aussenpolitik der Bundesrepublik Deutschland* (Bonn, Bonn Aktuell,
1989), pp. 177–8.

13 'Les projets de textes', *Le Monde,* 17 October 1991, Paragraph IV.3.
14 'Text der Erklärung des Regierungssprechers vor der Pressekonferenz',
    16 October 1991, courtesy of the German Embassy, London.
15 Statement by Foreign Minister Kinkel on 31 May 1992, AP press report,
    Bonn, Germany, 1 June 1992; Statement by Defence Minister Rühe on
    25 May 1992, 'Bonn a défendu le projet de corps franco-allemand',
    Le Monde, 28 May 1992; and slightly more ambiguously, Statement of
    Chancellor Kohl at La Rochelle, 22 May 1992, 'Conférence de presse
    conjointe de M. le Président da la République et de M. Helmut Kohl,
    Chancelier de la République Fédérale d'Allemagne', courtesy of the
    French Embassy, London.
16 Heinz Schulte, 'Cool reception for corps proposal', *Jane's Defence
    Weekly,* 9 November 1990; Annika Savill, 'Undermining the pillars of an
    alliance', *Independent* 22 May 1992; Michael Evans, 'Birth of Euro-army
    spurs Nato unease', *The Times,* 21 May 1992; William Drozdiak, 'Paris–
    Washington chill reflects wider split on Alliance's future', *International
    Herald Tribune,* 27 May 1992.
17 Roger Jiménez, 'Apoyo pleno de González a la propuesta defensiva París-
    Bonn', *La Vanguardia,* 20 October 1991; Miguel González, 'González
    propone que el futuro ejército europea sirva tambien a la OTAN', *El Pais,*
    22 October 1991.
18 'Belgien und Spanien am Korps interessiert', *Die Welt,* 18 November
    1991; 'Français, Allemands et Belges jouent à l'armée européenne', *Le
    Monde,* 24/25 November 1991.
19 'Aufstellungsstab für das Eurocorps nimmt Arbeit auf' quotes the figure
    50,000; earlier press reports talked of 100,000. But at the summit of La
    Rochelle, the figure of 35,000 was mentioned.
20 In the late winter/early spring of 1992, there had been other letters, such as
    the letter by Reginald Bartholomew from the State Department – now US
    ambassador to NATO – addressed to the European governments, which
    had already caused considerable irritation; see *Welt am Sonntag,* 24 May
    1992.
21 Hella Pick, 'Bush challenges Nato allies over keeping US defence role in
    Europe', *Guardian,* 8 November 1991.
22 Treaty on European Union, Title V, Article J.4 and Declaration of the
    WEU, Maastricht, December 1991.
23 Kurt Kister, 'Kinkel verteidigt das Eurocorps', *Süddeutsche Zeitung,*

2 July 1992.

24 Hans Binnendijk, 'How NATO+EC+WEU can equal security for Europeans', *International Herald Tribune,* 2 April 1991.

25 David Buchan and David White, 'Joxe urges bigger French rôle in NATO', *Financial Times,* 30 September 1992.

26 David Buchan, 'Wörner presses France to take bigger Nato role', *Financial Times,* 27 April 1993.

27 'Paris "engineering Nato collapse"', *The Times,* 6 December 1994; Patrick Cockburn, 'French "plot to split Nato over crisis"', *Independent,* 6 December 1994.

28 Nicholas Timmins, 'US move "signals end of Nato"', *Independent,* 14 November 1994.

29 Daniel Vernet, 'Nouveau pas de Paris vers l'OTAN', *Le Monde,* 11 March 1993.

30 'Eurocorps in NATO eingebunden', *Süddeutsche Zeitung,* 22 January 1993.

31 'Un entretien avec M. Alain Juppé', *Le Monde,* 6 March 1993.

32 'Un entretien avec François Léotard', *Le Monde,* 13 May 1993.

33 Jacques Isnard, 'La France siège désormais avec voix délibérative au comité militaire de l'OTAN', *Le Monde,* 14 May 1993.

34 'M. Léotard prône "une attitude nouvelle de la France dans une OTAN rénovée"', *Le Monde,* 25 October 1993.

35 *Livre Blanc sur la Défense 1994* (Paris: La Documentation Française, 1994), pp. 55–7.

36 'Le ministre français de la défense participera à une réunion de l'OTAN', *Le Monde,* 6 September 1994.

37 François Léotard, 'La sécurité européenne', *Le Figaro,* 30 September 1994; see also Jean-Marie Guéhenno, 'France and the WEU', *NATO Review* (October 1994).

38 P.L., 'France revient dans le giron atlantique', *Le Soir,* 6 December 1995.

39 'Discours du Président de la République, M. Jacques Chirac, devant le Congrès des Etats-Unis d'Amérique', Washington, DC, 1 February 1996, *Statements*, SFC/96/32.

40 Agence France Presse, 'Union de l'Europe Occidentale', 7 November 1995.

41 Pierre Lellouche, Deputy in the French National Assembly's RPR, made this proposal at the beginning of 1996, cf. Rüdiger Moniac, 'Eurokorps als Grundstein für Verteidigungsidentität', *Die Welt,* 1 February 1996.

42 Outlined by Britain at a special WEU meeting in London in February 1996, 'Großbritannien gegen Integration der WEU', *Frankfurter Allgemeine Zeitung,* 6 December 1995. See also 'A new NATO', *The Economist,* 9 December 1995 and Alyson J. K. Bailes, 'Sécurité européenne: le point de vue britannique', *Politique étrangère,* 60/1 (Spring 1995).

43 Reuters, 'Western European Union', 5 December 1995. Cutileiro was commenting on action in Bosnia, but he might as well have been talking about European defence in general.

44 Interview, Ottawa, Department of Foreign Affairs and International Trade, 11 December 1995.

45 The Gaullist consensus of the Fifth Republic stands in stark contrast here with the otherwise universalist tradition of France, see Beatrice Heuser, 'Mitterrand's Gaullism: Cold War policies for the post-Cold War world', in Antonio Varsori (ed.), *Europe 1945–1990: the End of an Era* (New York: St Martin's Press, 1993).

46 'Study advises pulling out of NATO', *Jane's Defence Weekly*, 26 March 1996; Seth Cropsey, 'The case for abolishing NATO', *Wall Street Journal*, 20 December 1994; see also Francis Fukuyama, 'For the Atlantic Allies today, a fraying of the sense of moral community', *International Herald Tribune*, 6 June 1994.

47 Albert Wohlstetter, 'Alternatives to negotiating genocide', *Wall Street Journal*, 12 May 1995.

48 'Clinton on troop use: "strategic interests" at stake', *International Herald Tribune*, 29 November 1995.

49 Martin Walker, 'America is coming home', *Guardian*, 25 May 1993.

50 Daniel Williams and John M. Goshko, 'A lesser U.S. role in the world? Official's remarks bring a prompt White House denial', *International Herald Tribune*, 27 May 1993.

51 Joann Byrd, 'Lost in Brand X murk at Foggy Bottom', *International Herald Tribune*, 2 June 1993.

52 Brent Scowcroft, 'America: the mission is new leadership for a new deterrence', *International Herald Tribune*, 5 July 1993; James Baker, 'President must restore America's role as world leader', *The Times*, 12 July 1993; George Brock, 'While Clinton dithers, NATO withers', *Wall Street Journal*, 26 July 1993; Fritz Wirth, 'Rückzug einer Weltmacht', *Die Welt*, 27 July 1993; Brent Scowcroft and Arnold Kramer, 'Going it alone and multilateralism aren't leadership', *International Herald Tribune*, 4-5 February 1995; 'Clinton: leadership role vital to US security, prosperity', Remarks to Freedom House (6 October 1995), USIS.

53 The White House, 'A national security strategy of engagement and enlargement' (February 1995).

54 Frederick Bonnart, 'A Europeanized alliance could play a vital role', *International Herald Tribune*, 10 November 1995; Stéphanie Marchand, 'Europe centrale: les limites de l'engagement américain', *Le Figaro*, 8/9 January 1994; Lawrence Freedman, 'Europe must prepare to lead the new Nato', *Observer*, 4 December 1994.

55 John Palmer, 'Anxious Finns and Swedes look to Nato', *Guardian*, 27 October 1992.

56 'Allocution du Premier Ministre, M. Alain Juppé, devant l'Institut des Hautes Etudes de Défense Nationale', 6 September 1995, *France Statements*, distributed by French Embassy, London.

57 Renaud Girard interviewed Charles Millon, 'Otan: Charles Millon veut un "état-major européen"', *Le Figaro*, 25 December 1995.

58 Pierre Haski; 'Chirac joue l'entrisme dans l'Alliance', *Libération*, 17 January 1996.

59 On the issue of defence-industrial competition, see Pierre De Vestel, *Defence Markets and Industries in Europe: Time for Political Decisions?* Chaillot Papers No. 21 (Paris: WEU Institute for Security Studies, November 1995); Jean-Hughes Monier, 'Vers une politique européenne concertée en matière d'armement', *L'Année européenne* (1995), pp. 86–91.

60 Andrew Moravcsik, 'The European armaments industry at the crossroads', *Survival*, 32/1 (January–February 1990), pp. 65–85; see also Ron Smith, 'Defence procurement: a European identity?', *RUSI Journal*, 137/1 (February 1991), pp. 42–8.

61 Cf. François Chesnais and Claude Serfati, *L'Armement en France: genèse, ampleur et coût d'une industrie* (Luçon: Nathan, 1992).

62 David S. Yost, 'France and the Gulf War of 1990–1991: political-military lessons learned', *Journal of Strategic Studies*, 16/3 (September 1993), pp. 339–74.

63 Ibid.

64 'Les yeux dans le ciel', *Le Monde*, 8 July 1995.

65 Cf. François Heisbourg, *Les Volontaires de l'an 2000: pour une nouvelle politique de défense* (Paris: Balland, 1995), pp. 62–7.

66 Jacques Isnard, 'Un arsenal complet qui marque une volonté d'hégémonie'; Laurent Zecchini, 'La restructuration se poursuit dans l'industrie américaine de l'armement', *Le Monde*, 29 June 1995. See also Russell Hotten, 'Union calls for defence links to repel US invastion', *Independent*, 26 January 1996; Frédéric Pons, 'Avis de tempête dans l'armement', *Valeurs Actuelles*, 27 January 1996.

67 Jacques Isnard, 'Vers un pôle européen du renseignement militaire', *Le Monde*, 20 December 1995.

68 For a summary of the Anglo-Saxon vs. the French beliefs on trade, see Patrick Minford: 'Europa braucht Freihandel', and Gérard Lafay: 'Europa braucht Handelspolitik', both in *Die Zeit*, 12 April 1996.

Chapter 7: Agenda for the twenty-first century

1 Franz-Josef Strauss, 'Europe, America and NATO, *Survival*, 4/1 (January–February 1962), p. 8.

2 For a history of such proposals, see Elizabeth D. Sherwood, *Allies in Crisis* (New Haven, CT: Yale University Press, 1990).

3 Dr Helmut Kohl, 'United Germany in a Uniting Europe', Konrad
   Adenauer Lecture at St Antony's College, Oxford, 1992, distributed by the
   Konrad Adenauer Foundation, p. 7.

4 François Léotard, 'La sécurité européenne', *Le Figaro,* 30 September 1994.

5 Malcolm Rifkind, Secretary of State for Defence, 'The Atlantic Community', speech of 13 October 1994, text supplied by the British Ministry of
   Defence.

6 Joseph Fitchett, 'Western Europe proposes new trans-Atlantic Pact',
   International Herald Tribune, 7 February 1995. See also Alfred Dregger:
   'Ein "Transatlantischer Vertrag" ist nötig', *Die Welt,* 2 February 1995.

7 Speech to Belgian Royal Institute of International Relations in Brussels ,
   30 January 1995 and at the annual 'Wehrkunde' conference in Munich,
   February 1995. Text made available by the British Ministry of Defence.

8 Speech in Washington, DC, on 2 March 1995, Presse- und
   Informationsamt der Bundesregierung, *Bulletin No. 16*, 6 March 1995,
   p. 135.

9 Presse- und Informationsamt der Bundesregierung, *Bulletin No. 32*,
   24 April 1995, pp. 268–9.

10 'Kinkel will reform der EU–Außenpolitik', *Frankfurter Allgemeine
    Zeitung,* 13 October 1995.

11 See, e.g., Klaus Kinkel, 'Vision Europa wird Realität', *Die Welt,* 10 July
    1995.

12 'Allocution du Premier ministre, M. Alain Juppé, devant l'Institut des
    Hautes Etudes de Défense Nationale', 6 September 1995, in *France
    Statements*, distributed by French Embassy, London, 13 September 1995;
    'Discours du Président de la République, M. Jacques Chirac, devant le
    Congrès des Etats-Unis d'Amérique', Washington, DC, 1 February 1996,
    Statements, SFC/96/32.

13 Interviews, Ottawa, December 1995.

14 'Joint US–EU Action Plan' (3 December 1995) made available by the
    Public Affairs Office of the US mission to the EU.

15 Texts in *Europa Archiv,* 46/1, 10 January 1991.

Select bibliography

Allen, Harry Cranbrook, *The Anglo-American Predicament: The British Commonwealth, the United States and European Unity* (London: Macmillan, 1960).

Anderson, Stuart, *Race and Rapprochement: Anglo-Saxonism and Anglo-American Relations, 1895–1904* (London: Associated Universities Press. 1957).

Aron, Raymond, *République impériale: les Etats-Unis dans le monde, 1945–1972* (Paris: Calmann-Lévy, 1973).

Bousquet, Alain, *Les Américains sont-ils adultes?* (Paris: Hachette, 1968).

Campbell, Charles S., *From Revolution to Rapprochement: the United States and Great Britain, 1783–1900* (New York: John Wiley, 1974).

Cogan, Charles G., *Oldest Allies, Guarded Friends: The United States and France since 1940* (Westport, CT: Praeger, 1994).

Cox, Michael, *US Foreign Policy after the Cold War: Superpower without a Mission?* Chatham House Paper (London: Pinter for the RIIA, 1995).

Dimbleby, David and Reynolds, David, *An Ocean Apart: the Relationship between Britain and America in the 20th Century* (London: Hodder & Stoughton, 1988).

Duroselle, Jean-Bapstiste, *La France et les Etats-Unis des origines à nos jours* (Paris: Le Seuil, 1976).

Eayrs, James, *In Defence of Canada: Growing Up Allied* (Toronto: University of Toronto Press, 1980).

Etzold, Thomas H. and Gaddis, John Lewis, *Containment: Documents on American Policy and Strategy, 1945–1950* (New York: Columbia University Press, 1978).

Ferro, Marc, *De Gaulle et l'Amérique – une amitié tumultueuse* (Paris: Plon, 1973).

Gaddis, John Lewis, *Strategies of Containment* (New York: Oxford University Press, 1982).

Gantz, Nanette and John Roper (eds), *Towards a New Partnership: US–European Relations in the Post Cold War Era* (Paris: the Institute for Security Studies of the WEU, 1993).

Select bibliography

Garvin, J. L., *The Life of Joseph Chamberlain*, 3 vols (London: Macmillan, 1962-4).

Gordon, Philip, 'Recasting the Atlantic Alliance', *Survival* 38/1 (spring 1996), pp. 32-57.

Heater, Derek, *National Self-Determination: Woodrow Wilson and his Legacy* (Basingstoke: Macmillan, 1994).

Kelleher, Catherine McArdle, *The Future of European Security : An Interim Assessment* (Washington, DC: Brookings, 1995).

Knock, Thomas J., *To End All Wars: Woodrow Wilson and the Quest for a New World Order* (New York: Oxford University Press, 1993).

Louis, Wm. Roger and Owen, Roger (eds), *Suez, 1956: The Crisis and its Consequences* (Oxford: Clarendon Press, 1989).

Martin, Laurence Woodward, *Peace without Victory: Woodrow Wilson and the British Liberals* (New Haven, CT: Yale University Press, 1958).

McNaught, Kenneth, *The Penguin History of Canada* (4th edn, London and Harmondsworth: Penguin, 1988).

Miller, John Donald Bruce, *The Commonwealth and the World* (3rd edn, London: Duckworth, 1965).

Palmer, Robert, *The Age of the Democratic Revolution: A Political History of Europe and America, 1760–1800*, 2 vols (Princeton, NJ: Princeton University Press, 1959 and 1964).

Remond, René, *Les Etats-Unis devant l' opinion française, 1815–1852*, 2 vols (Paris, 1962).

Rothwell, Victor, *Britain and the Cold War, 1941–1947* (London: Jonathan Cape, 1982).

Silberschmidt, Max, *The United States and Europe: Rivals and Partners* (London: Thames and Hudson, 1972).

Skard, Sigmund, *The American Myth and the European Mind* (Philadelphia: University of Philadelphia Press, 1961).

Smyser, W. R., *Germany and America* (Boulder, CO: Westview Press, 1993).

Steinberg, James B., *'An Ever Closer Union': European Integration and its Implications for the Future of U.S.–European Relations* (Santa Monica, CA: RAND, 1993).

Thibau, Jacques, *La France colonisée* (Paris: Flammarion, 1980).

Varsori, Antonio (ed.), *Europe 1945–1990s: The End of an Era?* (London: Macmillan, 1995).